make a shift, change your life:

Simple Solutions to Transform Your Life from Drab to Fab Now!

by karen rauch carter

Illustrated by Karen Rauch Carter

Make a Shift, Change Your Life by Karen Rauch Carter
Published by Exquisite Living Press

Publishing services provided by Pedernales Publishing, LLC
www.pedernalespublishing.com

Cover Art by Spiffing Covers
http://www.spiffingcovers.com

Library of Congress Control Number: 2013948821

ISBN 978-0-9898978-0-8 Paperback Edition
ISBN 978-0-9898978-1-5 Digital Edition

Printed in the United States of America

Testimonials from Clients

Wow—where to start . . . .

Karen has helped me through 6 moves in the last 11 years—from being a renter, to short stays in foreign countries for work, to buying and selling a home—and she's always "right on" when it comes to the challenges of where to situate belongings and how to "clear the space" of each new place . . . . The front doors have been in many different locations, and orienting the *bagua* has been a challenge for me, but she always knows exactly how to help! I can't wait to take her feng shui certification course some day, to learn more myself and be able to share it with others!

—Julie W., Ojai, CA

Karen's "Mindset Makeover" was such a huge help for me! She was able to help me with obstacles from my past that I just could not deal with on my own! It felt like the weight of the world was taken off my shoulders. I'm so much happier and more at peace now after my consultation!

—Barbara W.

About one week after you came, I won the 50/50 split at my children's school fundraiser. I won around $6,000!!! Plus, I am sitting here at my new desk with about six movie deals about to close. We went to our meeting that Friday, and not only did the studios agree on the one movie to do together as a group, but now they are putting together a slate of six projects to do together—potentially even nine. Holy smokes!!

Woohoo—with me and my husband producing all of them! It was much better than I could have dreamed. Seriously, a lot has happened.

The other piece of news is that my husband was offered a much larger office in the building, so we need to get his office squared away. He hasn't moved just yet, but it's in the works. It will be a temporary office until they are able to move it again to the other side of the building.

My friends are all going to be calling you. We are having way too much flow for them not to want in on it, too!!!!

—Stephanie G.

I've read *Move Your Stuff, Change Your Life* several times, but nothing compares to having Karen walk through your house!!! I finally contacted Karen after we had our very own 911 emergency with our youngest child, who was 17 months at the time. We had moved houses that year and a LOT seemed to be in disarray, but that was my breaking point.

My husband and I have three children ages 5, 3, and 2, and we both work full time. I was constantly feeling like I was doing it all by myself, overwhelmed, and like everything with the kids and home were all on my shoulders. Karen pointed out that none or very little of the "helpful" ch'i was making it down the hallway and around the corner into our living spaces or to me. Karen had me hang a crystal from the ceiling at that corner to help the *ch'i* round the corner. I never would have thought it was that corner in my Children and Creativity *bagua* where I needed a crystal to feel the Help—amazing!

That same night, my husband started doing the dishes, I was folding laundry, and my two oldest jumped in and said they wanted to help. So I started feeling the help immediately, and I'm VERY happy to say it has continued in big ways!!! This one crystal is a life saver to me and my family!

—Jennifer B., Indiana

Gosh, it's very hard to sum up in a short blip what I've gotten out of feng shui over the last 15 years . . . but here goes. "From helping me turn around a bankrupt restaurant in 12 weeks to helping me transcend personal lifelong roadblocks, Karen Rauch Carter's books and personal consultations have changed my life."

Feng shui is not magic; YOU are. Let Karen unlock your magic!

—*Kerry O'Hare, Texas*

When I fixed my prosperity corner of the house, in the mail within two weeks I received $300 and it upped to $4,600 in the mail by way of school and a car settlement . . . totally unexpected. Changing my house around made my life so much better. I didn't have to buy anything. Karen just moved stuff in my house and helped me put a red line in the back of my house, and oh my gosh—a lot of good things in my life came full circle. I also had a "Mindset Makeover" from her, and I started not being so locked in my house and was able to go out and enjoy the world. I even moved to a richer area and out of my mom's house.

—*Mark Reyes, California*

Dedication

To all my clients, who trusted me enough to grant me full access to all areas of their lives. That access allowed me to hone and distill the wisdom found in this book.

To all the readers of this book—I applaud you for your courage to change and your willingness to step up your vibration level. By helping yourself, you help the world.

And finally, even though we're midway through the teenage years, you are *still* my favorite distraction while writing, Cole.

Acknowledgements

I am filled with gratitude for the special people in my life who contributed to the creation of this book. I consider these souls my "evolution partners." Thanks to championing editor Cara Cantarella, best friend and unofficial "talk-me-off-the-ledge" design director Donna Allen, Anne Ricci and all my friends who gave input on design and content, and of course, all the many teachers and trainers great and small, who have passed on their techniques, ideas, wisdom, and conversations which became the seeds that bloomed into the content of this book. A partial list includes *the late Grand Master Lin Yun, Nate Batoon, William Spear, Roger Green, Robert Gray, Jan Cisek, Chris Howard, Larry Gust, Alison Armstrong, Dan O'Hara, and Dr. and Reverend Marge Britt.*

I am also grateful for each seemingly unconnected life experience that got me right here—at a place where I am able to share my thoughts and ideas, and hopefully be of service to whoever reads this book.

Contents

How to Use this Book

Consider this a self-guided workshop where you'll be doing some reading, some writing, some inner-reflection, and some physical work. And, well, for those of you who know me and my quirky writing sense of humor, the "Frankie" comments that organically showed up while writing are just there to keep it light. Life is serious enough, right?

Although the book is divided into Mind, Environment, Body, and Spirit sections, the techniques inside them "cross-pollinate"—they all affect each other. It's a holographic universe, so you really can't put a shifting technique into an exclusive, singular box. I organized the book in four sections to emphasize the "driving catalyst" for the particular changes you might be working on. However, all of the approaches reinforce and build upon each other.

Although it is perfectly possible to skip around and work the techniques that you feel best suit you without regard to their order, I do recommend familiarizing yourself with all of the techniques rather than assuming you know which ones will do the trick for you. Maybe, just maybe, you will respond to a particular technique from a section that you would not have expected to be all that important to you.

Here are a few recommended steps before you start:

1. Get a nice notebook for taking notes, completing exercises, and tracking your shifts. Also, have a pretty writing journal on hand.

2. Take photos of every space you live and work in now, before you change anything. Take at least one picture per room, if you can get a sense of the room in one shot. Also, take a photo of yourself. It may seem odd or useless to do this now, but these "before pictures" will blow your mind later when you see how far you've come.
3. Have an open state of mind and a hopeful or inquisitive attitude while reading and working through the techniques in the book. Your perspective adds yet another layer of good energy to support your changes.

make a shift,
change your life

Introduction

It's just a hunch, but if you take the time to open a book entitled *Make a Shift, Change Your Life*, you're probably thinking that some part of your life could be improved in some way. Hey, we've all felt victimized, stuck, scared, sad, hopeless, or some other uneasy feeling along the way. I'm certainly no exception. Here's a partial list of moments from my life's School of Hard Knocks that caused me to search out self-help books, workshops, and ways to change my life:

- Lost about 10 of my 100 classmates before I turned 20 from deaths due to separate random events, which caused me to doubt the sanity of the universe.
- Was slipped a rufi in college and to this day still have no idea what happened to my body for an entire night, which made me feel scared and untrusting.
- Moved across the country all by myself where I knew no one, for what turned out to be a horrible, misrepresented job that drained me of what little money I had and made me feel fooled, tricked, and stuck.
- Died and was brought back to life in a hospital after having a severe allergic reaction to a nut, which made me feel confused, scared, and paranoid. (One peanut could take me out?)

- Gained instant psychic abilities from the allergic-reaction event, which caused me to doubt my own sanity during what I call my "I hear dead people" phase.
- Married a guy who had serious family issues, in my opinion, which caused me to feel trapped.

Could I have stayed stuck, feeling victimized about any of those experiences? Sure. But thankfully, I ran across the following life-shifting methods, techniques, and practices that have allowed me to live not as a victim of the past, or even as a victim of current circumstances, but as a centered, content, healthy, and fulfilled human being . . . for the most part. In other words, I still use these shifters when I need to get back to being the real me—a beneficial presence in the universe—as opposed to the Type A, "human doing," complaining spaz that my ego would prefer for some wacked-out reason.

> In the past, I used to think of myself as a victim, but upon further review, I've decided that I was just a human.

The way I see it, as long as you're kicking, you can improve yourself either mentally, physically, or spiritually so you can benefit the universe with your unique presence. And from what I "got" when I was in the hereafter that day when I ate that nut and died, that's the whole reason we're here in the first place. But you have to be willing to change.

Life is like a NASA space mission: it involves a near-constant series of course corrections. Yep—those astronauts were literally "off course" over 90 percent of the time, but they wound up where they wanted to be due to the following:

1. their willingness to commit to actually going;
2. their willingness to not stop or turn around when they got off course; and

3. their willingness to correct their course over and over, not thinking of veering off course as a failure, but as part of the journey.

So, have I mastered life? No. Does everything always go the way I want it to go? No. But I can tell you that when I stay centered, trust my gut, and don't let the "off-course" times drag me away from my commitment to being an unlimited spiritual being, I taste the fruits of my efforts and enjoy the sweetness of life.

If you are willing to join me by shifting your mind, body, spirit, and environment to discover and align yourself with your ultimate divine nature, you too can enjoy the sweetness of life while you're on this journey. With the techniques in this book, you'll shift the very visible and invisible, internal and external, finite and infinite things that can take you (back) to a "happy place." Because it really is about doing things that eventually make you feel better, somehow or in some way.

Everything in your life that you find upsetting is an opportunity to help yourself choose to be centered and happy again, no matter if money, love, health, or any other woe is your source of unhappiness. With the following tools, you can manifest everything from deeper spiritual growth to a fun new car or a loving relationship. It's really your choice.

It is my vision for you that after reading this book, you'll have the confidence to use the tips, methods, and techniques provided to guide yourself toward a steady course of happiness throughout your life. You'll be your own happy and healthy life designer, consistently engaging in the processes that lead back to love, joy, and bliss in every situation.

There are many paths to life improvement out there. The techniques in this book happen to be the ones I have found to create quality change in my life and in the lives of hundreds of clients. They are my most used, go-to formulas—the tools in my trusty tool bag.

> Feng shui is a method of arranging your living environments so that they fully support your life in every way. The traditional feng shui term for a shift or solution is a *cure*. It is a visible or invisible change to your environment intended to bring about a change in your life.

For those of you who know me as a feng shui consultant only because you've read my book *Move Your Stuff, Change Your Life*, you'll soon see that not all of my "tools" are traditional feng shui techniques. While I am a devoted and respectful feng shui practitioner, I won't hesitate to share solutions from other traditions when I feel they can help you obtain results—thus the "healthy lifestyle designer" addition to my title.

As you read on, you'll learn one technique or method at a time, kind of like trying on different pairs of glasses. One pair will help you see something new from one perspective—then you'll change glasses and see how that same issue is connected to and can be helped by a completely different approach. Some tips you'll understand and work through in about two seconds, while others will ask more of you before results appear. In the end, you'll have your own trusty tool bag to use on any occasion.

Whether you feel like your life is hummin' along just fine or is in desperate need of a major overhaul, this book has something to offer as you grow along the way. So, grab your notebook again—we've got stuff to do!

One more thought before we continue . . . .

Commit and It Will Be Shown to You

There's a great quote worth pondering from Sir William Murray that speaks to the magic and power of commitment.

> *Until one is committed there is hesitancy, the chance to draw back, always ineffectiveness. Concerning all acts of initiative and creation there is one elementary truth, the ignorance of which kills countless ideas and splendid plans: that the moment one definitely commits oneself, then Providence moves too. All sorts of things occur to help one that would otherwise never have occurred. A whole stream of events issues from the decision, raising in one's favor all manner of unforseen incidents and meetings and material assistance, which no one could have dreamt would have come their way.*
>
> —*Sir William Murray*

Providence, as defined by Webster's, is "the benevolent guidance of God or nature." So, in a nutshell, when you "definitely commit," you will be guided to achieve that which you've become committed to. Yeah! You don't have to "do it all yourself!" God, the universe, energy, nature, or whatever you want to call it will be working right beside you, clearing the way. That's nice to know, eh?

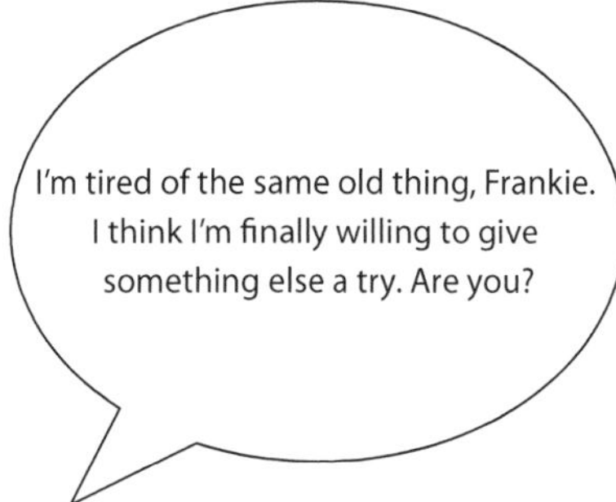

Commit now to taking action on at least some of the wisdom in this book. Commit to a willingness to change. Commit to shifting your current life to a better one in some way. Commit to having fun in the process. Commit fully, and it will be shown to you. Committing is like getting free rocket fuel as you travel toward your destination. So, my first tip for you is: COMMIT!

> If you always do what you've always done, you always get what you've always gotten.

Chapter 1: Prepare for the Shifts

All of the shifting techniques and suggestions to come follow at least one, if not all, of the following premises. So, be open to them. Jot them in your notebook if that helps them soak in. It's OK if you don't believe or understand them now. I still don't understand gravity or how a radio functions, but that doesn't stop them from working in my life.

Basic Premises

What's going on in your life is a direct reflection of what's going on in your mind, body, spiritual connection, and/or environment.

Believe it or not, there is a direct and often quite literal translation between your life situation and your beliefs, perceptions, the stuff that surrounds you, and the stuff you put inside you. Take your living environment, for example. The poor guy doesn't live in a castle, and the king doesn't live in a cardboard box. Your environment also reflects how you see yourself, how you respect yourself, your beliefs about how you should be treated, your beliefs about money, your spiritual beliefs and faith, and so on. They are all interconnected. If something changes with any of these, the changed element affects the others.

What's closest to you has the most impact on you.

What do you notice more often, the color of the ocean floor off the coast of Antarctica, or the color of your bedroom? How about the wood of the trees in the rainforest or the wood of the floors in your house? So, what do you think affects you more on a day-to-day basis—the wild monkey habitat of the Amazon or the human habitat called home?

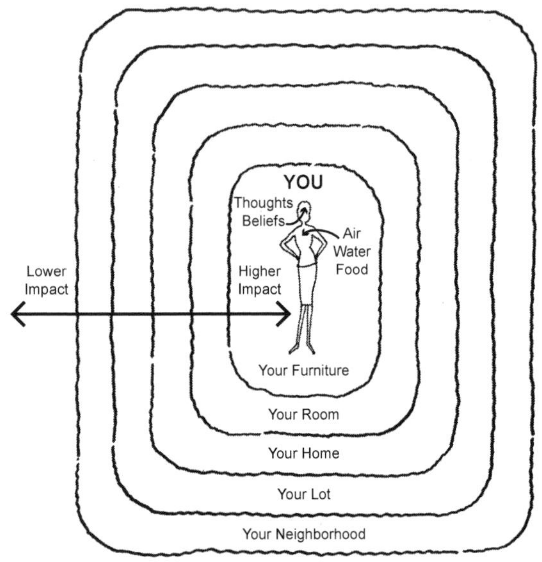

What's closest to you has the most impact on you

Figure 1

The universe—somehow, some way—supports our little planet called Earth hovering here in space. The Earth supports the countries, and the countries support the cities, and the cities support the neighborhoods. The neighborhoods support your lot, and the lot supports your house or building. The house or building supports the rooms, the rooms support the furniture, and the furniture supports

YOU! You can also look at the stuff actually inside your body—food, air, water, etc.—as REALLY close stuff that affects you.

And let's not forget about your thoughts and beliefs, because like food and air, they're inside you somewhere, too! Your outer environment and life circumstances are definitely a direct reflection of your thoughts and beliefs as well. Consider thoughts to be real things—as energetically real as your bed or toothbrush. They make a huge impact one way or another when it comes to how your life shows up. I'm certainly not suggesting that people forget about faraway places like Antarctica or the Amazon. I'm sure that if we saw and felt a more immediate, short-term effect from saving the planet than from fixing up our houses, we as a nation would probably be shopping at Save-the-World Depot instead of Home Depot. I'm simply trying to convince you that your immediate surroundings and the changes you make to them can have the greatest and most immediate impact on your life *and* the life of the planet in turn.

The fortunate "ripple effect" of you "getting your shifts together" is that your local efforts help the global picture. Yes, your individual work is helping save the planet! Imagine what this world would be like if every individual tended to his or her own inner and outer environments in this way. You are literally "being the change you want to see in the world!"

> When considering a shift (or as a traditional feng shui consultant would say, "a cure"), try changing the closest impacting item first. An ordered list worth considering is: food, air, water, clothes, furniture, room, home, lot, neighborhood, etc. In other words, work your way out for stable support.

Seen or unseen, everything is energy—and it all affects you.

Not to get all wrapped up in science or anything, but scientists have proven that everything we see—and everything we don't—is made up of energy. So, if you organize both the seen and unseen environments to have optimal energy patterns for you, you will find yourself living a happier, healthier, more easily flowing life.

"Like energies" are attracted to each other.

If you've got a negative record playing over and over in your head making you feel bad or stuck, or if you are living in an unsupportive environment, you'll only attract experiences that match that level of negativity or lack of support. Conversely, if you've got a positive inner world and a supporting physical environment, you'll attract positive and life-supporting experiences. Remember this concept up ahead when you fear change or want to resist it. If you want something other than what you have, you've got to make a change. It's that simple.

Even if you aren't in a rut or stuck, if you decided to pick up this book, you have an intention to reinvigorate your life. If you're afraid of the word "change," use the word *exchange* instead. I invite you to exchange the unhappy parts of your partially happy life for a consistently happy one!

> You have to give up the life you have to get the life you want.

Nothing about your life situation or circumstances can change unless you change the way you see yourself.

Transformation is as much about changing the inside to match the outside as it is the other way around. In order to get results, you must accept responsibility for your own thoughts and believe that it is possible to change. (The next chapter has a technique to help you if this is a challenge.)

> In order to change your current space or situation, consider changing your mind about it.

Where thoughts go, energy flows.

You've just learned that everything is made up of energy. But here's one idea you might not have heard: energy is conscious, and it is connected to and reacts to thoughts and feelings. Ask a physicist: they'll tell you that the outcomes of their subatomic experiments are influenced by the consciousness of the observer. This news can be good or bad for you, simply depending on how you judge your thoughts and feelings. If you don't like your current thoughts and feelings, don't worry—you'll soon learn ways to change them. But do start paying attention to the rambling thoughts that flow by. They may need to be de-cluttered, because *energy follows thoughts and feelings.*

It's always good in the end. If it's not good now, it's just not the end.

This is a reminder that there may be fallout when the energy "changes tracks" by you abruptly changing your mind, or putting your attention on something else. Just know that to get your Dream Life train going in another direction, you might stir up some dust. Consider this an invitation to look at any "negative" fallout as something potentially positive for your future, even though it may be very unclear in the moment how that could possibly be true.

So, when you see a little dust, remain calm. Check in with yourself and see it as a sign that your hard work is about to pay off!

Anything is possible.

I promise you, I've seen miracles. Don't limit yourself. Some of you will report instantaneous results, while for others change may take a little time. It's really up to you. I've seen gals have babies after being told by doctors that there was no way for them to get pregnant, and I've seen the family "black sheep" welcomed back into the clan—both with very little effort. I've even seen one woman with zero shoulder mobility for over three years regain full motion in less than six weeks without the surgery that the doctors insisted was necessary by shifting four items in her outer environment: we removed a knife from her night stand, changed her bed and desk location, and stopped the "energy leak" flowing from her giant ocean view living room window. Yes, anything is possible.

When in doubt, feel free to experiment.

With the right intentions, you can hardly go wrong. Experiment with your shifts. If a change doesn't appear to be working, consider modifying the change or revising your thoughts about it. Remember, thoughts are things too, and sometimes they need to be adjusted.

Build Your Personal Map to Happiness

Similar to planning vacation travel, you need to know where you are now and where you want to go to arrive at the correct destination.

To help you move toward your "better future," throughout this book you'll investigate the categories of mind, environment, body, and spirit. Some information is from the visible world (like the stuff in your bedroom and the food you eat), and some resides in the invisible world (thoughts, beliefs, and feelings). You'll mine information from both realms to complete your planning and shifting work.

And then, when actually making your shifts, you can either start with the "matter" side of things and change your outer environment in order to bring about a feel-good change in life, or you can simply work on your own intangible thoughts, beliefs, and feelings to get your life circumstances and material world to transform before your eyes. Either approach will work, as will working on both simultaneously. You choose. Whatever method you believe to be fastest for you will be. But you have to start by clearly deciding what you *really* desire.

What Do You Desire? What Is Your Dream Outcome?

The reason for using the following self-help techniques is to change something to fulfill a desire, so eventually you will feel better in some way. It's more the *feeling* behind it that you're after than the stuff itself. Let's face it, even if you were using these tools to manifest a new bike, you'd ultimately want to feel safe and empowered to have a faster method of transportation than walking. You'd want to feel good about how much easier the new method has made your life. And because it's the feelings you're ultimately going for, as a first step you must identify the feelings you'd like to create.

Are you clear on how you would want to feel if you indeed changed your life for the better? If not, take a moment to start a list of these feelings. Write down your dream destination—your Dream Life scenario. Ask yourself, "Why did I buy this book?" or "Why did my friend give me this book?" if it was a gift.

Write "My Dream Outcome" in your notebook and then answer the following question. Where do you ultimately see yourself, and by when? For example, would you like to be more patient, more loving, or more consistently devoted to a meditation practice? How about being a wealthy philanthropist who feels great about sharing his or her fortune? Or is it a loving, trusting, nurturing relationship that you wish you had?

> If you've been able to imagine the worst, then you can imagine the best!

Go ahead—dream big! Go wild! Sizzle with enthusiasm while dreaming! Your imagination muscle may be tiny and atrophied, and it may take a little time to find, but trust that it is there. If you are struggling to create your list, jot down the first five things that pop into your head that would immediately put a smile on your face. If a Genie came out of a bottle to grant all of your life's wishes, what would they be?

Organize your wishes in a priority list, or just let them flow and randomly appear on the page. Don't worry, there are no wrong answers—they're your dreams! It doesn't matter if you don't know the first step to take to achieve them right now. Give up any limiting notions, and just *be* with your dreams.

If you still have no clue how to dream, make a "complaint list" of all the things you know you don't want. Then write down the opposite of each item on the list. That's your working Dream List for now.

Dream Feelings

The next step after listing your dreams is to make sure every one has a specific feeling attached to it. What exact feelings do you want to have in your Dream Life? Do you really want a stash of paper bills and metal coins, or do you want to feel safe, free, and tingling with delight over all the things your money can buy?

As I stated earlier, *energy follows thoughts and feelings*, and *like energies are attracted to each other*. If you can connect with the thought and feeling energy of what it's like in your Dream Life, then you are building within your inner environment the map to get you there. Powerful and positive feelings such as gratitude, love, passion, excitement, joy, anticipation, tenderness, and compassion are much more likely to attract happiness-generating energy than are feelings of victimization, lack, destruction, apathy, and shame. Those feelings usually steer you in the other direction.

Once you've identified your Dream List and feelings, re-write your list in such a way that you are *in* your dreams and can feel them.

When you write this out, take some time to dream about your physical surroundings as well. Are you working in an office in your ideal scenario, instead of at the warehouse where you currently work? Are the kids' bedrooms de-cluttered and organized? Does the landscaping feel supple and alive?

Here are a few examples of wild dreams that include feelings and surroundings:

Relationship - "I am in a fun, loving relationship where I feel cherished and adored! We share so many special moments of love for each other—especially in our eco-friendly "lover's retreat" bedroom that we created together. It's like I constantly walk around on a dreamy love cloud, the way we are so physically attracted to each other. I find myself giggling all the time, and I always feel so safe, nurtured, cherished, and happy! Our relationship brings out the best in me."

Prosperity - "I've got a fire hose of riches always raining down on me, and I happily accept it. That old paradigm of working hard for money has been shattered. It's just not true—and the funny thing is—it never was. I'm excited that I finally woke up to that false belief. I feel blessed to continually have the financial freedom to do anything I want. My home is so welcoming, clean, organized, and beautiful; I am grateful to have it and honored to share it with others. Life is such a fun adventure!"

Health - "I feel great from head to toe! My body is centered, balanced, and working in a state of peak performance. I feel energetic and full of vitality! I am so elated that I'm not only physically healthy, but mentally and emotionally balanced as well! The retreat wing of my home is so restful and rejuvenating with the waterfall, thriving plants, and all the beautiful sunlight—just being in it energizes me. I feel spiritually connected there as well, which also makes me feel centered and serene throughout my day."

Career/Life Path - "I am so excited that I have found my place in the world! It is a joy to get out of bed, go to the most awesome 'office' on the planet called 'a lounge chair on the beach,' and make a huge difference in the world while I sit in my tee shirt and shorts. I had no idea that a career could be so spiritually and financially rewarding at the same time. It feels so wonderful to be paid so handsomely for having so much fun. I love my richly fulfilling life! Thank you, Universe!"

The magic behind this whole exercise is this: the power of the universe doesn't distinguish between what has really happened to you and what's just a thought or a dream. You can bring just as much awesome energy toward you by feeling great about something in your dreams as you can by feeling great about something that has really happened.

> The universe always delivers the equivalent of whatever feeling vibe you're emitting.

Remember, the key is your "feeling vibration." If you're moping around feeling victimized and full of shame, you will attract experiences that energetically match that vibration. Conversely, a joyful vibe will attract opportunities that energetically hang out at the same level as joy. This writing out of your dreams is what you're going to review later on as you track your results from this book, so don't skimp!

Where Are You Now?

Now that you've spent some time considering what feelings and physical surroundings you ultimately want to have in your Dream Life, pause and take a look at your visible and invisible starting points. Where are you now? How do you feel at the moment? What do your home and work place look and feel like now? Write these observations in your notebook under the heading "Where I Am Now."

First, take a look at your physical surroundings—especially the places that are closest to you over the most amount of time. Do your living and work spaces reflect how you desire to live? Do they work well for you and inspire the feelings you wrote in your ultimate imagined life?

Walk throughout your living spaces (both inside and outside), and write down your perceptions. Is your space nice? Does it tell someone else's story, because everything was given to you? Does it appear neat, while "behind the scenes" it's a cluttered mess? Is it fresh, happy, and healthy looking? Observe it as if you are a visitor who has come to find the person you wrote about in your Dream Outcome list. Do your spaces reflect THAT person?

List any observations you notice. For example, "the dining room looks more like a home office than a real dining room," or "the bedroom feels depressing with the stained carpet and dusty drapes." What stands out as a definite no-no with regard to that dreamed-up life you wrote about? Perceive the spaces with all five of your senses. List anything that bugs you for any reason, even if you don't know why. Be sure to look in the refrigerator and food cabinets and at the quality of your food, dishes, pots, and pans, as this information will be valuable for the Body section later on.

Once the living locations are done, do the same for your workplace.

Now, get in touch with the invisible part of the equation. Break out the intangible "feeling" qualities that describe where you are right now. Here's a list to get the ball rolling: Shameful, guilt-ridden, depressed, apathetic, afraid, optimistic, anxious, indifferent, empathetic, forgiving, neutral, regretful, humiliated, embarrassed, serene, loving, blissful, accepting, full of rage, grieving, joyful. The more you can shed light on and identify these intangible feelings, the easier it will be to change them. Take a look back at your assessment of where you are now, or take a moment with the list above and sit quietly and see if any emotions pop up that you did not list previously.

Finally, take a moment to assess your spiritual connection, however it appears to you. There is no specific religion involved here unless you make it so. Do you feel spiritually bankrupt? Is this the one category that feels aligned in your life? Have you never had a "higher connection" but wished you did? Did that life you want to shift toward include being "in the flow" and feeling like a part of the greater universe? Sit with it and then complete your writing for now.

OK, prep work done. Let's get your shift together!

Chapter 2: Modernize Your Mind

In order to dream up your Dream Outcome, you had to be able to actually use your mind and think it, right? Like I said, that imagination muscle may be tiny and atrophied, but it is there! This chapter is all about fine tuning "the muscle of the mind" so you can attract, embody, and live that dream. Yes, you're going to de-flab that mind of yours from any unhealthy "stinking thinking" and exercise it in a way that leads you to consistently positive thoughts that *continuously* support your dream. Heck, after some of these exercises, you may feel the urge to re-think, stretch, or even completely upgrade your dream! Your "little engine that could if only . . ." mind is now going to become "the little engine that could" mind, period.

Welcome to the Modernize Your Mind Gym. Grab your water bottle and a towel—we've got work to do.

If you get confused at any time during the following exercises, get excited! Because confusion precedes a new order in the mind! Yeah! New order brings new opportunities. (You ARE looking for new opportunities in some part of your life, right?)

The Climbing the Ladder of Emotions Modernizer

If your Dream Outcome imaginings have you thriving in a loving relationship, feeling wonderfully healthy, or being wildly generous because of your new-found wealth—but you're having a hard time snapping your finger and feeling those ultimate emotions as you write—consider taking a more realistic journey to get there by climbing the ladder of emotions.

In his book *Power vs. Force*, Dr. David Hawkins laid out a list of emotions that he calibrated for vibration level using applied kinesiology.[1] For example, the lowest-vibrating emotion he could find was shame/humiliation, and the highest was the ineffable emotion of enlightenment. Imagine each feeling as a musical note on a scale ranked from low to high. Figure 2 is an illustration of what the feelings might look like.

According to Hawkins, every emotion or feeling carries with it a specific energetic charge, vibration, or value. Positive emotions are open and flowing, while negative emotions are stagnant, stopping the flow. He states that any time you're feeling positive emotions, you're allowing in what you desire—and any time you feel the negative emotions, you're blocking out what you want. In the illustration, I have placed the positive-vibrating emotions above the line and the negative-energy attracting ones below. The key is to keep yourself aligned with the positive emotions that attract your dreams, instead of blocking or repelling them.

Chances are in identifying your goals, you've written down many of the emotions that are quite high on the scale, such as love, harmony, joy, and passion. But how do you get to the higher emotions from where you are now? Can you just jump from apathy to bliss? Or from rage to contentment? According to the Abraham-Hicks teachings and their similar "emotional guidance scale," it usually is challenging. Like running a marathon without training, there's usually too large of a gap between where you are and your goal to jump right there.[2]

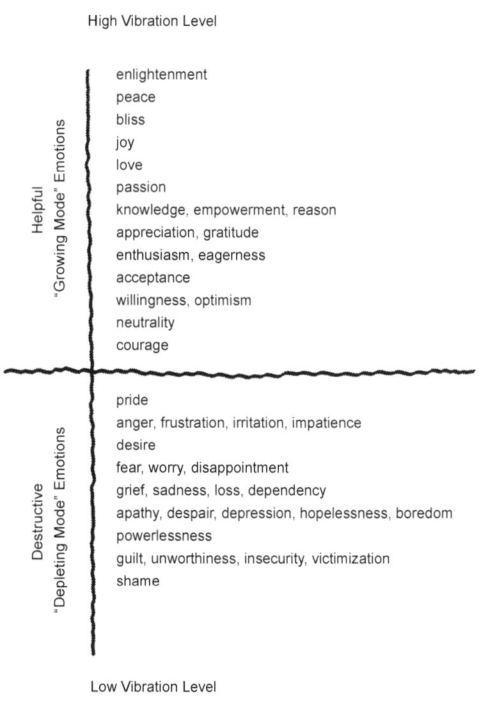

Vibration Chart of Emotions
Figure 2

But perhaps while you can't get there immediately, you *can* get there over time. In order to "shift" your mental environment, you must first de-clutter it of toxic thoughts and beliefs. Then you can enhance it with thoughts and beliefs that uplift you and support the life you are building. Your uplifting thoughts, perceptions, and beliefs can be awesome shifters for the mind. As you gradually improve your vibration, you will be able to stay at the higher levels of emotion for longer periods of time. Soon the feelings of love and passion will be deeply rooted in you, instead of just desires on your Dream List.

The goal is to be aware of your usual level of thinking, and to do something to change it if it is not the energetic level you wish to attract.

Do you know the emotional level where you most often reside? Can you see the importance of shifting your thoughts and feelings?

I'm betting you didn't write down "anger" as a goal feeling on your Dream Outcome list, but if the majority of your thoughts are at the emotional level of "apathy," perhaps you should consider it. Compared to apathy, anger is actually a higher-quality energetic vibration. It could literally serve as a stepping stone to get you closer to a positive emotion such as courage. There are many people throughout history who had to get angry enough to step into a "change-the-world," take-action role.[3]

Any bits of time spent in the presence of the higher-energy states can help pull you toward those states more permanently by attracting life opportunities that inspire those higher-quality feelings. So, even if you can't muster up the feelings yourself, get yourself physically near someone or some group that can. Go to RahRah conferences. Watch feel-good videos online. Like attracts like, remember? If you become conscious of the feeling, you'll feel it. And then it can raise your vibe.

On the other hand, if you're *impatiently itching* to get to the top the high-vibe list, you're hanging out down low on the list. Your impatience itself is a lower vibe. Take a deep breath, relax, and give yourself permission and the time to stair-step up the list. Are you *willing* (higher vibration) to try? Even moving up one small step at a time is progress. As you shift slowly, keep your sights on two vibrations that may help you most to achieve the life of your dreams. These are love and gratitude.

Love

In an ultimate universe, if I could choose one emotional energy vibe for you to hang out in, it would be love. I'm not talking about that seemingly ever-elusive, pride-filled love that comes and goes as our mood shifts about another person or situation. I'm talking about a constant, unwavering state of being that originates from the heart.

Love is the fuel behind a growing and thriving life. It is the most efficient energy for shifting your life from drab to fab, period. In a nutshell, if you dig around anything beneficial, you will unearth love somewhere in the process. But it's often hard to blink and be there, I'll admit. So, if you can't "go there" yet, look down the emotions list a little bit. Perhaps try gratitude.

Gratitude

Gratitude is *definitely* doable, and it will without a doubt take you toward your goals. Gratitude is defined by Webster's as "thankful appreciation for favors received." In order to experience gratitude, you must appreciate something.

Appreciation is defined as a "sensitive awareness." The term aware is defined as "knowing, realizing, or conscious." In other words, to get to gratitude, you must first be conscious. Hey, being conscious—now THAT sounds doable!

Next, appreciate stuff: be conscious that you are holding a sensitive awareness of something. Practice seeing everything as a "favor received." In other words, look around and appreciate what's in your life right now. Instead of wallowing around in a pity pot, put a "silver lining" on everything you think about.

If your inner voice just said something like, "oh, brother" when you read the silver lining part, or if you feel that there truly is nothing to be thankful for, you've got a negative belief system that needs work. We'll deal with that in a minute. Take a moment right now to stop and breathe. Close your eyes and take a big, deep breath. Can you muster up any thankful feelings for that free breath of air? What if you had to pay for every breath? Isn't it amazing that there's always air for everyone to breathe on this planet? Close your eyes again and calmly contemplate this until you feel some kind of a shift. Slooow doooown. Breathe.

This exercise might truly feel uncomfortable for those who usually wallow around in "cup half empty" land and "victim-hood." If this is you, then step back and twist things around until you can find something to be thankful for. Lost your job? Appreciate that you had the opportunity to work there for however long you did and the fact that you are now free to explore other opportunities. Lost your home or a loved one? Appreciate the memories now. Have health challenges? Appreciate the "challenge" and commit to the possibility of changing it. Appreciate that this book is illustrating how to learn to appreciate!

"Favors received" may be a sunny day, a glance at a beautiful flower, or an awareness that you are alive today. It doesn't simply mean a traditional favor that another person does for you. If you are really having a hard time getting started with this exercise, concentrate on nature first. Spend time using your senses to experience nature. Try soaking in something naturally beautiful: smell a plant, feel a stone, watch a cloud, or take in a sunset until you feel your vibe shifting toward appreciation. (For double points, notice how you are breathing when you do.) Then consciously be thankful that you had the opportunity to experience this.

Now we're stoking the gratitude fire! Feel what happens to your body when you express gratitude. Perhaps it is a slight smile, perhaps your shoulders melt down a bit, or maybe your breathing mellows out. Notice it and be thankful that you are given signs that you are being grateful. Wallow in gratitude—that's something worth doing.

Take a look back at your notes describing what you desire. Appreciate your past self who was just struggling to get clear on what "the Dream Life" looked like. Be thankful for the dream!

> Gratitude is the fuel source for love. Love is the most efficient energy for accomplishing anything.

The 4 Questions for Clarity Modernizer

Here's a "training wheel" exercise to get the ball rolling if you are in the grip of indecision or aren't entirely sure exactly what you want. Some call these questions "Cartesian Questions," as they are predicated on

René Descartes' 17th century Cartesian logic and can be graphed in four quadrants like the Cartesian coordinate system in math. But there's no need to graph anything. Just write out the answers to find clarity.[4]

Consider the context of the issue you are confused about or an action you may be thinking about taking. Then write down the answers to the following four questions:

1. What would happen if I did?
2. What would happen if I didn't?
3. What *wouldn't* happen if I did?
4. What *wouldn't* happen if I didn't?

For example, let's say that on your Dream Outcome list, you wrote "Get a College Degree in Fine Arts." Run that dream through these four questions to see if you indeed are willing to go the distance with it. Once again, there's no need to know every step necessary to get you there, as Providence will be doing its part.

Perhaps on the "What *Wouldn't* Happen if I Did?" list, you might write, "Because of the commute, I would not have the quality time with my kids that I do now." OK, then. Armed with more clarity, you can choose to move forward with the goal, not do it, delay it until after the kids are grown, or take an online course that does not require a commute. Whatever you decide, there will be no more frustration or guilt about not doing it and feeling like you "never get what you want" or you "never finish anything." You will be taking a conscious stand and choosing not to be a victim of life circumstances or any other "bad feeling" around this "unfulfilled dream." The conscious act of simply unhooking or releasing the often unconscious, negative thought patterns is a powerful first step on the path to manifesting your dreams.

The 4 Questions for Clarity might need to be tweaked a bit to fit your issue exactly, but you can unearth all sorts of limiting thoughts and beliefs about what is stopping you from having your Dream Outcome in life. There is serenity in clarity. There is peace in deciding to do or not do something with clarity. Validate yourself by contemplating the answers to these questions and then modifying your actions around them. If you see a belief problem or issue, just keep reading. There are many Modernizers up ahead to help you handle them.

The Helpful People Box Modernizer

Once you've gotten clarity on what you want, you may need help accomplishing it. The Helpful People Box cure from my book *Move Your Stuff, Change Your Life* was such a hit (based on the number of people e-mailing me their success stories) that I just had to include it in this book as well. Here is one such story that came my way:

> *I am really shocked. I am doing a major cleaning/purging of stuff in my house, and my idea was to Feng Shui each area as I went, but I got a little anxious and decided to start a Helpful People Box. I put in the name of a friend I just couldn't get ahold of and the name of my husband. I had to—I was getting so frustrated with having to do everything by myself. Two days later, he did the dishes (third time all year), took out the trash, cooked dinner, went grocery shopping, and even picked up the floor after our baby—using the vacuum cleaner, which he's never, ever done. It was so above and beyond the call of duty, it just had to be the Feng Shui.*
>
> *The same night, my friend who I couldn't get ahold of called me. OK, she NEVER calls. This was the third time she has called me in maybe FIVE years. You could have knocked me over with a feather at that point. Wow.*

> *If these had happened on different days, I probably wouldn't have believed it was the Feng Shui, but it's too coincidental to ignore. I am just in shock. THANK YOU for writing the book in such an easy-to-use way. I really appreciate it.*
>
> —*Susan*

What have you got to lose, right? It's an odd little cure, but this sucker produces results!

Get a metal box or any metal container with a lid. (Even an aluminum foil-covered envelope or container will work.) In the box, place a handwritten note of thanks, as if your dream has already come true and you have received the help you need. As we saw above, you can simply put the names of the people you want help from in the box as well.

Also, you get bonus points if you can really *feel* in your body that your request has come true when you write it. Let's say, for example, that you are looking for a successful surgery outcome. You could write something like, "Thank you for providing me with the perfect hospital staff who performed my fully successful surgery. I recovered quickly and effortlessly and was consistently pain-free throughout the process." Place this note in your box. For extra feng shui bonus points, you could place the box in the front right-hand part of your room or home, based on where you walk into the room or home, or even on the right side of your desk.

Once you have done this modernizing "ritual," get into the mindset that you have placed your order and there's no need to worry about it again. Just like you don't fret wondering if the cooks in a restaurant forgot or aren't making your food after you order, once you make your Helpful People "order," all you have to do is wait for it to "be done."

Confidently knowing that it will happen when the time is right is the best way to proceed when you use the Helpful People Box Modernizer.

Here are some additional Helpful People Box rules:

1. You can add multiple "help requests" to the box at one time.
2. Once an item comes to fruition, you can simply remove that item from the box with great gratitude and discard it.
3. You may place long-term and more general requests in the box, such as "airlines are always helpful to me."

The Dream Diary Modernizer

Sometimes you may be looking for more than supportive people to help a dream come true, particularly if your dreams involve major shifts in many areas of your life. That's when you might use the Dream Diary Modernizer. If you think that diaries are just for dreamy teenage girls, think again! This Modernizer puts a spin on the average diary that shifts your life *fast*. I'd even go so far as to say "in less than six weeks." (Oh, yeah—I said it!) Here's what you do:

Imagine each day how your perfect day goes in your dreams. Write down what you imagine. Pretend you are writing a diary—writing it just as if it had happened or is happening now in real life. Here's an example:

> "Today, I woke up in my soul mate's arms. He's such a wonderful husband to me! We giggled as we looked into each other's eyes, because we still can't believe that we found each other. I feel so safe and comfortable and yet excited and sexy all at the same time . . . somehow like my life makes perfect sense, now that we're together. I always feel like a kid who's practically jumping out of her chair waiting to open

up a big pile of birthday gifts. It's this feeling of anticipation that makes me wiggle with excitement on the outside, but gives me a feeling of being always safe to show my excitement on the inside. It is soooo nice. My cheeks just got red now simply remembering it!

We got up and opened the shutters to see the wonderful ocean view before going downstairs to a scrumptious breakfast laid out for us by our personal chef, Danny. It is so wonderful to have him cooking for us now. I always have healthy, well-balanced meals now, and I feel great because of it.

After breakfast, we took our morning walk down by the shore before we got ready to "work." My driver makes sure I am always where I need to be at the right time. What a load off my shoulders not having to worry about the schedule!

I love my job as a host of a TV show. Everyone loves the show, from the ad buyers to the producers and crew to the viewers: everyone is happy. It's so cool that I get to do this TV show that helps so many people in need as well. I feel honored to go to work each day—it energizes me like a good workout!

Once I got home, I was greeted with a lovely meal on the veranda with my loving

> husband. Our total absorption with each other was apparent as we conversed, not even knowing that the table had been cleared. We sank into the hot tub to catch the sunset out over the ocean and both breathed a big sigh as we realized how unbelievably lucky we are.
>
> I called a good friend to catch up for a bit and to schedule some one-on-one time before getting ready for bed. I am so grateful for my awesome family and friends. It warms my heart to be connected to so many wonderful people.
>
> I close this day spooning with my adorable, charming, and darling husband. But the spooning doesn't last long. Oh, the passion we have once in bed! I never knew what the word "soul mate" actually meant before meeting my adorable husband, but I get it now. Not only are we physically and emotionally bonded, but we're spiritually connected as well. Our hearts seem melded together. We give thanks for the opportunity to live this lifetime together. What a great day. What a great life. My cup of joy overflows."

Got it? Write down how your day went, as if you lived it. If this feels strange at first, give it time. Nurture yourself, and then, as calmly as you can, start to imagine baby steps until the full-on dream starts feeling real in your mind, and the dream feelings are real in your body.

The more specific you can make your dream, the better. Look up words in a thesaurus if you're having trouble finding the right way to express the emotions you are literally feeling during this process.

After you write each "feeling sentence," stop and take a moment to figure out where in your body you felt those emotions. Did feeling *safe* make your shoulders drop a bit? Did *wonderful* make you feel your face smile? Did *warm* feel tingly in your chest? Notice where you actually felt that feeling you just wrote down. Spend time feeling that feeling again before moving on. The more time you spend feeling specific feelings, the more quickly you will find yourself in a position to feel them "in real life."

You can write down the entire day first and then go back and read it through, taking the time to explore the feelings if you want, or you can feel the feelings along the way as you write. It doesn't matter. What does matter is that you start rolling your "energy snowball" by experiencing the feelings in your body that you wish to feel in your Dream Life.

WARNING: Be careful what you wish for in this Dream Diary! No clients of mine who committed to writing it daily made it to Week Seven without a BIG CHANGE in their life that propelled them toward their actual dreams in the diary. I will tell you also that one day, I *literally lived* one of the Dream Days in my diary exactly as I wrote it. The day had seemed so over-the-top, I didn't think the stuff I wrote was actually possible!

Oh, yes—and you can also store your Dream Diary in your Helpful People Box or in the front, right-hand part of your room or home (based upon where you enter) for added measure.

The Plan the Party Modernizer

This Modernizer is one of my favorites to use when my clients are facing legal situations, and man-oh-man, has it come through. You can use it for other types of problems, but I really recommend using this method when you are completely butting heads with someone and you can't get your feelings unhooked from the situation.

Clients Cindy and Drew were in a mess. They had a long-time, "trusted" employee who not only had embezzled funds from their business, but also was living in one of their homes and wouldn't move out. There were several lawsuits filed, and my clients were a wreck. Cindy came to me saying that by the time the actual court date came around, they would have already lost the house to the bank because the "squatting embezzler" wasn't paying rent anymore. She thought there was no way out.

So, what did we do? We planned the "It-All-Worked-Out-Fairly-and-In-Our-Favor" party. Crazy-sounding, yes—but VERY EFFECTIVE! When you plan an "It's-All-Over-and-We-Won" party, you are literally picking a date and literally having a party. This is not a pretend party or exercise. This is a real party, even though the outcome has not happened yet. In Cindy's case, we needed to choose what seemed like an extremely unreasonable date for the party (literally like five months before they were going to trial).

She thought I was crazy, but she stuck with me. We discussed the food, the dishes, the music, the invitation list, the invitations, you name it—and she started to work. Every time she started wavering and doubting, or feeling disdain for the person she was suing, I got her back on track with the party planning. In doing this, I was helping her to cut off her energy attachments to the situation and not feed the negative snowball effect.

So here's what happened. We started planning all of this on a Friday, and literally that following Monday, Cindy's attorney got a call from the opposing attorney requesting a settlement. They went before a judge—within the week—and the judge ruled NOT in my client's favor! Cindy FREAKED! She wasn't even out of the courtroom when she called me screaming, "We lost!!!"

You know what I said? I said, "Stay the course. You've got good feng shui, and if we've gotten that kind of result so far by pushing the whole thing forward, it HAS to come out in your favor, because it's working!" Yes, she thought I was crazy again. But still she stuck with it.

Here's what happened next. When the judge wrote up his decision, he did a complete 180 and ruled in HER favor! Cindy's attorney told her not to get excited about the decision, because there must be some mistake. But there was no mistake—she won. How crazy is that?

When you see this technique work as often as I have, you get kind of confident—even when all indicators say you're nuts! I've got other juicy stories just like this one, so believe me, the Plan the Party Modernizer works! Now go party!

Write a letter of forgiveness to the person or organization that you are fighting. Don't worry. You don't have to send it to them. You can burn it after you are through if you want. It is just a ritual to further unhook your energy field from theirs. Trust me, I know I'm asking for the moon here: if someone is suing you or vice-versa, it is very hard to forgive them. But if you can sit quietly and find the wherewithal to do this, it will pay off.

Try imagining them as a fellow character in a play. The two of you are at odds with each other on stage, but once you are off, you go back to being two people without a grudge at all. Make your mind work for you in this modernizing manner, and you'll score big.

The Ol' Switcharoo Modernizer

In this Modernizer, you isolate the benefits of events you once saw as negative and focus your attention on those instead of the "bad stuff."

To start, write down at least three events in your life that began in a way that you would describe as "very negative," but ended up giving you something very valuable, such as insight, wisdom, monetary gain, a relationship, a child, or a more fulfilling career. As a matter of fact, you might realize as you write, if it wasn't for this event, those valuable things would probably not be in your life today. As you write the events down, be sure to also note the negative way you felt when they occurred—angry, sad, hurt, guilty, frustrated, overwhelmed, fearful, etc.—as well as the positive emotions that you now have because of these events. One more thing: for each event, note how much time passed between when you viewed the event as negative and when you saw it as positive.

Once this is done, AND ONLY when it's done, proceed with the following steps.

1. In your notebook, list every scenario in your life that you think SHOULD be different than it is. At least, list your most pressing scenarios for now. Be patient with yourself as you complete this step.
2. Once you complete your list, look at each item one by one and ask yourself, "am I SURE that this scenario should be different?" In other words, are you 100% certain that it SHOULD BE some way other than what it is? Could it instead possibly be giving you gifts and benefits, just as it is? Could it be providing you with lessons and wisdom that could prove vital in your future?
3. Look back to that first list of three events that you wrote, and notice how long it took for you to reframe a "once negative" as a positive. Then, look at the current list of "shoulds," and ask yourself if it is possible that you are just in the "between time," and that once ENOUGH time has gone by, you will see this as something positive. Remind yourself of the premise we saw in the first chapter: "it's always good in the end—if it's not good now, it's just not the end." Can you shake yourself out of your dug-in stance on this event enough to consider this?

When I was 23 years old, I "died and came back" from an allergic reaction. I had never heard of the term "near-death experience" at the time, but now that I have heard of it, I still think my description is more accurate because it wasn't "near" anything! It WAS a death experience.

For years, I labeled that event as "the worst thing that ever happened to me." (In reality, what was actually "the worst" was the coming back part, but try telling THAT to people who haven't gone through this!) I milked that story for years. It was like my personal trump card for story-telling. "Oh yeah? Well, I died! Beat that!"

Then, after eventually becoming a feng shui consultant—that's right, *Move Your Stuff, Change Your Life* and this book would have never been around if I wasn't kicked back here to live in this body again—I ran into many clients who were grieving. And luckily for me, I could confidently have a conversation about death with them and actually help relieve some of their pain and grief.

And then it hit me. My "dying and coming back" experience wasn't the worst thing that ever happened to me—it was the BEST thing that ever happened to me. Not only could I help those who were grieving, but I also understood how feng shui cures could work IMMEDIATELY, because I remembered experiencing the state of "no time." WHAT A BLESSING that whole dying event was! It took me years to turn that one around.

Using the Ol' Switcharoo technique, I have seen plenty of my clients snap out of it and completely change their minds about how to describe negative events in their lives. I had one client who wanted a new man, a new car, and a new job scream "I hate feng shui, I hate feng shui, I hate feng shui!" at me when, after pulling an all-nighter making feng shui changes, she immediately totaled her car, broke up with her boyfriend, and got laid off. But she was just on the fast track. Within six weeks, she had a better job, the car of her dreams, and a new man. Know what her story was then? "I love feng shui, I love feng shui, I love feng shui!" That's what!

Take that list of "shoulds" and place it somewhere where you will see it often. Then, whenever you notice it, pull the Ol' Switcheroo by filling your body with excitement and saying, "I am present to the presents of these situations in my life now."

The Belief and Your Body Modernizer

As I stated earlier, the universe doesn't care if your feelings are created from a real event or an imagined one. Now it's time to look at what those feelings are actually doing to your body. Scientists now know that feelings literally affect your physical health and create the energy-matching circumstances *AND FEELINGS* that show up in your life. Just as Dr. David Hawkins studied the vibration of emotions, cellular biologist Bruce Lipton, Ph.D. spent years studying how low-vibrational emotions affect our physical bodies. Lipton classified all emotions into three cell-affecting groups: helpful or supporting life, harmful or depleting life, and neutral. And they can't be in more than one category. He also noted that what triggers cells to be helped or harmed depends solely upon **your perception** of what is going on in your environment.[5]

For example, if the body interprets the environment as hazardous to its health—if the environment is an abusive situation, perhaps—it sends signals with that information into the cells. The cells respond by "going into protection mode," which is energy-depleting rather than helpful to the body. "Depleting" may look like constricted blood flow to the vital organs so as much blood as possible is available for the muscles to run away, or simply constipation or diarrhea, for example. How long the body can sustain itself in this mode depends entirely on the availability of its resources.

So, when you perceive or use your senses of sight, taste, touch, smell, and hearing, you are judging whether your surroundings are good or bad, safe or unsafe, health-generating or health-depleting, and so on. And your physical body is changed by these judgments.

All individuals have their own unique perceptions of what's going on around them. Someone else experiencing the same event might have a completely opposite perception of or reaction to it, similar to how siblings who were brought up in the same family often have very different perceptions of their upbringing.

Review the physical environment items in your "Where I Am Now" list from Chapter 1. What objects in your living environment—now, or in the past even—appear to trigger "depleting-mode reactions" that, according to Dr. Lipton, are harming you at the cellular level? You may be surprised (or not) to know that even sometimes family, friends, symbols, and the media make this list of depleting triggers.

Let's take a look at the media, for example. Back in the olden days, prior to mass media influence, our "environment" was perceived as considerably smaller than it is today. But now, thanks to satellites, the Internet, and competition in the media industry, we are inundated with information that results in dive-in-the-ditch, protection-mode, depleting perceptions all day long. It feels like that war, shooting, or murder is literally right there in front of you, thanks to the media's "good coverage." You can see it with your own eyes and hear it with your own ears—just as if you were there.

Similar to experiencing a "dream that felt so real," each time you expose your senses to this type of stimulus, they download a perception—usually one of tragedy, loss, victimization, insecurity, vulnerability, fear, or another low-vibrating emotion—which of course puts you in that ol' depleting protection mode. Yes folks, thanks to technology, the entire world (and then some) has become our immediate "fight or flight" environment. That bombing over there makes you feel unsafe over here. That fire, tornado, flood, hurricane, tsunami, or volcano way over there causes your stress level to go up and is actually nipping at your life—even though you are out of harm's way. Can you see the viscous cycle that's been created? (I'll spare you the rant about shoot-'em-up video games.)

It may sound like I'm promoting cold-heartedness and ignorance of world events, but I'm not. I'm simply showing you a potential unhealthy or deadly negative influence in your environment. The problem isn't the media *per se*. Only you can decide what your perceptions are and what feelings and beliefs are generated by events in the world around you.

> Spend more time thinking about or doing what makes you feel high-vibrating feelings, and shift your attitude away from the things and people that make you feel lousy.

Now, let's look at things from an environmental perspective. Consider the symbols you have in your living and work places (or perhaps in your vehicle). In addition to limiting or ending your exposure to the people and media sources mentioned above, remove tangible items from your living and working environments that usually bring about a cellular-depleting reaction. For example, I have found that removing the following "destruction-causing" stuff from homes and workplaces or where much time is spent always improves the lives of my clients in spite of their connections with these objects.

- Skulls
- Weapons
- Low-vibrational addictions such as drugs, alcohol, and cigarettes
- Words, music, or symbols about conflict, war, murder, death, or destruction

And just like there's no difference between your body's reaction to a real or imagined threat, whether you have the physical items, or merely the symbols of them around you, there appears to be little difference in the results as well. A gun painted in a piece of art carries almost the same energetic value as a real gun, for instance. And why would this be so hard to believe? If a nightmare can get your heart pounding and tears running down your face, a symbol of something negative in your space can too—at the unconscious level, perhaps, but it can.

I had a client who had in his home, among other things, skulls, skeletons, modern and medieval weapons (real and in art), bats, gargoyles, cigarettes in art, bondage items, and mummies—oh, I could go on—and who told me that there weren't 15 minutes that went by that he didn't have to work hard to stay off drugs. Desperate enough to not lose custody of his daughter, he gave me *carte blanche* to completely overhaul his house while he was away for a week.

I tossed every negative symbol I could find in the house and completely refurnished and painted the inside of the home. I space cleared and did many of the things in the upcoming Environment chapter as well. It went from looking like MegaDeath lived there to looking like the home of a healthy, wholesome family.

When my client returned, he literally wept, he was so happy. His energy definitely shifted right before my eyes. And after about 4 weeks, I checked in with him and he said, "Honestly, I have not thought about doing drugs since you did all this. I'm really amazed."

I'm telling you, symbols are powerful.

Hey, Frankie—why don't you get rid of that snowy lone wolf picture hanging over your bed to see if it helps to ignite a relationship for you?

So, the task for this Modernizer is simple. Remove any items with negative connotations that trigger low-vibrating feelings from your living and work spaces, and you will shift your life for the better—REALLY!

And if you are doubtful, remember the premise "Feel Free to Experiment!"

The Complaint Eradicator Modernizer

In the Belief and Your Body Modernizer, we focus on separating yourself from items and symbols in your environment that may trigger negative physical reactions. Next, here's a technique that literally connects the mind and the environment!

It is funny how we talk about our lives in architectural terms, and how we talk about our architecture as if it's a living being. We say "breaking the glass ceiling" when referring to women getting ahead in the workplace. And when we say we're "giving our house a face lift," it sounds as if we're going to call a plastic surgeon.

Personifying your living quarters—and actually treating your house like it's a good friend—is a very helpful exercise for Mind Modernizing purposes. It's in fact very wise to think of your home as a living entity. After all, if your eyes gave you the capacity to see things as detailed as if you were looking through a high-powered microscope, you would see that it *is* alive! All the molecules of your home and furnishings would be twirling around in front of you as if they were at a school dance. Is one view more real than the other? I think not!

Here are a few house "body parts," from a traditional feng shui perspective, to give you a better picture of your house as a living entity:

- Windows are considered the eyes of the house;
- Doors are the mouths;
- The exterior façade of the house is actually the skin of your house's body;
- Hallways and pedestrian circulation paths within the home are the home's circulation system;
- The attic or roof is equivalent to the house's head; and
- The "back" of the house will either be supporting it or not, just like the back and spine support a human body.

Every body part, organ, and system in your body is expressed somewhere in your home. We'll get into a few more of these house body parts later on; for now, it's just a good exercise for you to be able to picture your surroundings as a living, breathing entity. The living energy that your home holds is what you are trying to collect and get to support you and your life. Your task is to help that energy flow in the most life-affirming, prosperity-producing, relationship-building, happiness-generating vibrational patterns possible.

Instead of being frustrated by your inner or actual voiced complaints, use them to your advantage as guideposts or a call to action to make shifts in your living and work spaces. There is valuable information hidden within those complaints, because whatever you are complaining about will be expressed in those spaces—often quite literally. (If you've got someone in your life who's a big complainer, whip this empowering technique out on them and see what they think!) Your life will *definitely* change for the better if you take care of the constant negativity inside and around you.

Now that you've started building your personal map to happiness and are clear on the direction you wish to go, take one giant step toward it by quickly rearranging, removing, or reworking the stuff around you that mimics your constant or biggest complaints. For example, if your complaint is "I'm not as sharp as I used to be," or you simply want to maintain your mental "sharpness," sharpen all your knives, scissors, and other items that are supposed to be sharp. If there is no essence of sharpness in the home, there is no sharpness in your life. A knife that can't cut butter or a razor that can't cut stubble is not helping your mental sharpness—get it?

It is also helpful to enlist a friend or family member to help you with your complaint list. Ask them if they can identify any of your frequent complaints, and ask them for the exact words you use. Or take five minutes to sit down with them and ask them to write down your complaints as you rant, especially writing the key words or phrases you use that seem odd to them. Get it all out now and be quick about it, and then consider it done. There will be no more time and life wasted on stuff you don't want from here on.

Ellen's Curious Condition

Here's an example of how I connected the dots between one client's home and her curious health issue. The first thing I remember when Ellen opened her door to greet me was the condition of her hands. All of her fingers were bent over—kind of curled up like bird claws. On top of that, they were raw, pink, and oozing from some sort of eczema condition. Almost as soon as I took in this sight, I was hit with the most foul-smelling stench I have ever smelled in a home. My sinuses started burning immediately.

Upon entering, I quickly figured out that the smell was generated by the host of guinea pigs, hamsters, and rabbits—some caged and some running loose—inside the home. Her house was "oozing" (totally matching the state of her hands) with odor and the stench of feces. The house was not only cluttered with odor, it was physically cluttered with trash, food, piles of clothes, papers, and well, just about everything else you can imagine. Let's put it this way, I've never seen tufts of rabbit hair against interior house walls that looked like snow drifts before. The exterior was just as bad, with a landscape that had not been trimmed, mowed, or maintained in what looked like years. There were weeds that looked like rope-sized vines crawling up the façade (a.k.a. "skin") of the house.

As I was reviewing the home, I asked Ellen how long her hands had been like that. She said seven years. After she voiced her list of things she wanted me to help her shift with feng shui, we began walking through her home. In the bedroom, when I tried to open her bedroom dresser, I broke my fingernails because the drawer didn't budge when I pulled the handle. I quickly drew my hands back and suddenly noticed that my hands were literally in the same bird-claw shape as hers! I asked her how long she had had the dresser and she replied, "It was my husband's, and once we were married, it became my dresser." I asked her how long the drawers had been like that, and she said, "They've been *stiff* as long as I've had it." Of course, my next question was, "How long have you been married?" "Seven years," she replied.

If she hadn't been so overwhelmed with clutter and noxious fumes, it would have been a lightbulb moment for her. The word "stiff" was a big clue as to the problem with her hands. I personally find it more common for people to refer to drawers that don't open as "stuck." But it was stiff clutter, animal poop, drawers, doors, and windows for her, and stiff hands she had.

Are you stiff somewhere?

Common Complaints and Their Cures

Here are some of the most common complaints I have heard in consultations. To address them, I've listed the items in the home as well as the "inner environment" affirmations that might help mitigate the reason for the complaint.

"I'm stuck."

Outer environment review list:

- Remove clutter, especially anything that keeps doors from opening fully.
- Unstick any doors and windows that are stuck, including closet and cabinet doors.
- Move stuff in your house that has not been moved in a long time.
- Add something that moves to an overly still or stifled space, like a fan or a clock with a second hand.

Inner environment sample affirmation:

- "I flow effortlessly through life."

"I'm so drained all the time."

Outer environment review list:

- Check plumbing for any irregularities, especially drips and leaks, and repair these.
- Close drains that are not used on a daily basis.

Inner environment sample affirmation:

- "I always have the perfect energy available to me for any situation."

"I feel out of balance."

Outer environment review list:

- Repair any furniture that is wobbly, weak, or teetering, such as bookcases that are shaped like parallelograms rather than rectangles, four-legged chairs that have only three legs touching the floor, or office chairs and furnishings that have a wheel missing.
- Repair sidewalks and loose stones in paving.
- Review rooms to see if there is an imbalance of furnishings—for instance, all of the big, heavy pieces of furniture and the stone fireplace are on one side of a room, while the other side is empty or simply has a big glass window.
- Hang pictures straight on the walls and avoid a stair-step layout.
- Re-level a foundation where the floor is no longer level.

Inner environment sample affirmation:

- "I am even-keeled, confident, and trusting."

"I'm not seeing things clearly, and I've made some poor decisions."

Outer environment review list:

- Clean the TV, windows, computer monitor, windshield, and any other items that need to be viewed clearly.
- Repair any windows in your surroundings (car, home office, etc.). Remember, windows are the eyes of the environment!

Inner environment sample affirmation:

- "I see and think clearly and effectively. Insight for making good decisions always comes to me at the perfect time."

"I don't feel like I have a handle on the situation."

Outer environment review list:

- Repair any broken or loose door, drawer, or cabinet handles, knobs, and pulls.
- Check and repair handles on suitcases, briefcases, and purses.

Inner environment sample affirmation:

- "I always handle myself correctly and confidently in any situation."

"It's like I'm running into walls with whatever I do."

Outer environment review list:

- Look for walls immediately in front of you as you enter room doorways. If they are closer than you are tall, then hang a mirror on that wall so that you see yourself in the mirror (at least from your chest to about six inches above your head) instead of the wall. If the wall is just inside the front door, hang art that has a "distant view" in it on the wall straight ahead.

- Remove the wall if you can or are remodeling or rebuilding.
- Turn your desk around if you are sitting for many hours with a wall (or even a window) right in front of your face.

Inner environment sample affirmation:

- "I am always in contact with unlimited potential and opportunities."

"I keep getting tripped up . . . "

Outer environment review list:

- Repair any cracks or grade changes in sidewalks and hardscape outside.
- Complete maintenance necessary on steps (loose rugs, wobbly tread, etc.).

Inner environment sample affirmation:

- "I flow through situations and circumstances with ease."

"I feel crummy."

Outer environment review list:

- Sweep up the crumbs on the floor and from the cracks of the upholstered furniture.
- Clean out the refrigerator and food cabinets.

Inner environment sample affirmation:

- "My body, mind, and spirit are blissfully healthy and whole."

"I'm burned out."

Outer environment review list:

- Fix the pilot light on the stove or any other appliance, if it is broken.
- Check, clean, and repair the fireplace.
- Light a candle.

Inner environment sample affirmation:

- "The fire of life's passions burns eternally within me."

"I want more spice in my love life."

Outer environment review list:

- Put more spices in your spice cabinet.

Inner environment sample affirmation:

- "I always enjoy and experience a special spice in my love life."

"I can never find commitment in a relationship."

Outer environment review list:

- Commit to a style in your home's interior and exterior design.
- Make a commitment to nurture, love, and take care of your home.

Inner environment sample affirmation:

- "I celebrate the commitments in all the relationships in my life!"

"My money flows out as quickly as it comes in."

Outer environment review list:

- Repair leaks inside and out.
- Keep toilet lids down and bathroom doors closed.

Inner environment sample affirmation:

- "An ever-flowing and overflowing income is consistently maintained in my life!"

Please Help My Husband

Here's one of my favorites. One couple hired me to assess their situation, and while the three of us were walking through their home, the wife leaned in real close to me and whispered, **"Help my husband get his shit together!"** I stopped and said, "Where's all his shit?" (Hey—not my word choice, but it was hers and I had to go with it!) I then asked to see the bedroom closet. As I had suspected, she had taken over the entire double walk-in closet, and he had his belongings scattered here and there in little closets and cabinets all throughout the house and garage.

She was sorry she had mentioned it when I told her that a great cure for the situation was to allow him to place all his things together in the master closet where they were supposed to go! Do you see where we're going with this exercise? Stop, look, and listen. Then, make a shift.

The Energy Transfer Modernizer

This last Modernizer is a wonderfully profound hands-on technique (literally) that I use to help clients undo a false belief or perception that is standing between them and their dreams. I have seen it help my clients quickly break old, negative thought patterns, as well as empower them to move forward in their lives with confidence. I also consider this a good exercise to do when certain questions show up, such as "Why didn't my change-my-life efforts work?" or "How come feng shui works for everyone but me?"

There are two ways to perform the Energy Transfer exercise. The first takes three other people besides yourself; the second way you can do alone. I'd recommend giving the group method a try if you have three other people who you think would be willing participants. And use the one-person method as a fallback.

Group Energy Transfer Technique

The goal of the group technique is to receive energy from three friends who believe in something that you want to believe, but currently don't if you're being honest with yourself. (Need I say it? Don't choose people who can't muster up that belief for you!)

Start the process by choosing one item from your Dream Outcome list. As an example, let's pretend you want to work on finding a mate or relationship. Try to find the exact words that would describe the perfect relationship for you. Perhaps you want a relationship that is "honest, passionate, and fun." You can also use the feelings you attached to this dream. Maybe you said you wanted to feel loved, nurtured, and cherished in an honest, passionate, and fun relationship.

For more precise words, look in a thesaurus to pinpoint even more exactly what you want. Try to find words that have an emotional charge and make you feel something. Choose qualities that you may feel have eluded you forever, or qualities that you feel for some reason everyone else gets to have but you. Let's say that after the thesaurus exercise, you have now added "nurturing" and changed "honest" to "trustworthy." OK, now your attribute list is complete. You want a trustworthy, passionate, nurturing, and fun relationship. (I left off the feelings in this example for brevity.)

Next, ask yourself the following three questions about relationships using your word choices. You're going to be checking in internally to see how you answer these questions, either physically or through inner dialogue.

The three questions are:

1. *Is it possible* for me to have ________________ (fill in your descriptive phrase) *now?* Be sure to put the word "now" at the end of the question.
2. *Am I capable* of having ______________ (fill in again) *now?*
3. *Do I deserve* to have ________________ (fill in again) *now?*

Using the example above, the three questions would be: "Is it possible for me to have a trustworthy, passionate, nurturing, and fun relationship now? Am I capable of having a trustworthy, passionate, nurturing, and fun relationship now? Do I deserve to have trustworthy, passionate, nurturing, and fun relationship now?" Check in with yourself and feel what you believe about your questions. Does your inner dialogue say "No" or give you a sarcastic "Oh yeah, right!" response to any of these questions?

An alternative to asking yourself these three questions is to say them in statement form and see how much they feel like the truth or a lie. For example: "It is possible for me to have a trustworthy, passionate, nurturing, and fun relationship now. I am capable of having a trustworthy, passionate, nurturing, and fun relationship now. I deserve to have a trustworthy, passionate, nurturing, and fun relationship now." After stating the sentences aloud, feel how true they are for you. Did your inner dialogue immediately reply, "No, that's not true" when you said any of these lines?

The operative words here are "possible," "capable," "deserve," and "now." The words *possible*, *capable*, and *deserve* will ferret out any lies you have picked up along the way that are currently not allowing "the dream relationship" to show up for you. The word *now* at the end eliminates the possibility of the sentences becoming true because of some other limiting belief you have: "Well, sure it's possible as soon as I lose that weight, get that degree, save that money, blah, blah, blah."

Here's a little tip. If you feel it's true when you say, "It *is* possible for me to have _______________ now," and "I *am* capable of having ________________ now," and "I *do* deserve to have ______________________ now," but you don't actually have the desired outcome in your life, this means that you have not plugged the right adjectives into the sentences. Keep digging until you find the descriptive words that make at least one of the sentences not true. Perhaps you believe it is possible and that you deserve it, but you feel incapable of having that dream relationship. As long as at least *one* sentence feels untrue, you will get results from this exercise.

Before we go on, take a look back at those desires that you believe you are not capable of having, you do not deserve to have, or that it's not possible for you to have. Imagine going out to lunch with a good friend or family member who you love and saying to them, "Hon, it's not possible for you to have a trustworthy, passionate, nurturing, and fun relationship now." Or, "You're not capable of having a trustworthy, passionate, nurturing, and fun relationship now. " Or, "You don't deserve to have a trustworthy, passionate, nurturing, and fun relationship now." I mean, honestly, doesn't that seem like a cruel thing to say to your loved one? You are trying to consistently think high-vibrating, loving, and joyful thoughts, right? Well then, if it is so terrible to say something like that to a friend, why would you say it to yourself? If you had a friend who talked to you like you talk to you, how long would that friend still be your friend?

Back to the exercise. This is where you bring in your friends to help. (Make an energy-swapping party out of it by having everyone take a turn!) Remember, it is important that you choose people for this Modernizer who believe that it is possible, that you are capable, and that you are deserving of this relationship (or whatever), OK? We don't want your energy-givers saying "yeah, right!" in their heads about your situation, too. There's enough of that flying around! These people have to be full supporters of you and your dreams. They must hold the belief for you that what you want is possible for you to have, that you are capable of having it, and that you deserve to have it. As a matter of fact, strangers often work great as supporters for this Modernizer. They usually think everything is possible for you, that you are totally capable (why not?), and that you absolutely deserve all the things you want, because they haven't had time to create any false beliefs about you yet!

Your three friends or strangers should stand around you in such a way that one is on your left side, one is on the right, and one is directly in front of you. Each friend is the keeper of one of your three affirmations. One is the "possible" friend, one is the "capable" friend, and one is the "deserve" friend. (For example, put "possible" on the left, "capable" on the right, and "deserve" in front of you.)

Inform everyone of the words they'll be using in their statement ahead of time, so they can practice it a couple of times if they want. Sometimes people have so many adjectives in their affirmations that their support people get mixed up. If this happens, try doing the exercise a couple of times, using half of the adjectives the first time and half the next, until you feel that you've covered all of the adjectives and they all now feel true for you, or hold your list in front of you during the exercise so the energy givers can see it.

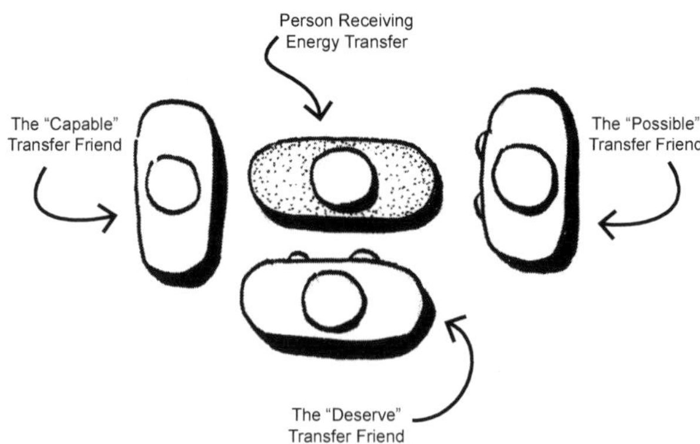

Group Energy Transfer Positions

Figure 3

With your friends standing all around you but not touching you, you say each of the three statements one time. "It is possible for me to have_Fill in______ now. I am capable of having __Fill in_____ now. I deserve to have ____Fill in___ now." The "possible" friend then touches your shoulder with her hand and says her line, "It is possible for you to have _Fill in_______ now." Then she puts her arm down. Next, the "capable" person puts her hand on your closest shoulder and says, "You are capable of having____Fill in_______ now" and then takes her hand off of your shoulder. Then the "deserve" friend places her hands on both of your shoulders, as she is right in front of you, and says, "You deserve to have _____Fill in_______ now."

Then, all three friends put their hands on your shoulders just like they did individually, and they each say their individual affirmation line over and over until they feel you've "got it." The three friends are saying their lines out loud on top of each other, so it sounds like a jumbled conversation. Each one of them is vying for your attention by possibly accenting different words in their line, or saying your name in front of their line: "SALLY! You deserve to have a trustworthy, passionate, nurturing, and fun relationship now!" followed by "Sally, you DESERVE to have a trustworthy, passionate, nurturing, and fun relationship NOW!"

It is the job of your support people to make you "take in" the sentence they are saying. It is your job to take the sentences in. If you know that you are an auditory learner, close your eyes and tune in to one friend at a time until you feel you "get it." If you are primarily visual, look at each friend one at a time until you feel that what they are saying is true. Take the statements in however you need to. Just allow them to come in. This information may feel uncomfortable to allow in. After all, you've been happy running around all this time holding on to a lie, and you're quite used to it. This exercise is replacing that idea, and egos don't usually take kindly to giving up their beliefs!

Some things that may happen during this exercise are:

The person who is receiving the affirmations giggles. I have observed that giggling is the ego's way of not allowing the information in. In this case, friends: don't stop saying your lines. The person is not finished taking them in.

It gets hot. Your intentions are gathering a charge. The vibration is speeding up. Friction causes heat. Sweating is a perfectly acceptable thing to do when helping a friend!

Tears flow. Sometimes it is hard to hear how capable you are or how deserving you are from loving friends. Let the tears flow. Do not hold them back. This is what mental de-cluttering looks like. Your old lie is physically releasing from your energy field. Tears are a good sign that things are going as planned.

Nausea. It's rare, but sometimes people will feel queasy in response to letting their old habits go. It appears that they have stored these habits or beliefs in their gut. This reaction is along the same lines as tears. Go with it. It's working.

Peace and calm. Sometimes you can physically see the lie leave by watching the face of the person you are "treating." It will soften and glow.

When the three friends stop saying their lines (this can happen all at once or at separate times, depending on when the friends feel that their sentence has been integrated), the three friends should slowly take their hands off of the receiver and gently put their hands back at their sides.

Next, the receiver of the energy transfer, with the three friends still around, says the three sentences as statements: "It is possible for me to Fill in____ now, I am capable of _____Fill in_____ now, and I deserve Fill in_____ now." The receiver must check in and see if the statements "feel true" now. If not, then perhaps another trip back to the thesaurus is in order, and a new group of adjectives can be used, but there should definitely be a shift.

That's it—you're finished! I cannot say enough about this exercise. It has saved the day many times for me and my clients.

Individual Energy Transfer Technique

If you want to go it alone, first figure out your adjectives by looking in the thesaurus just like in the group technique above. Then, affirm these adjectives in a sentence, like this: "A _Fill in_____ and I are one." Here are some examples:

- "A trustworthy, passionate, nurturing and fun relationship and I are one."
- "Optimal health and I are one."
- "A career that is financially rewarding, creatively inspiring, and environmentally loving and I are one."
- "Consistent, obligation-free financial freedom and I are one."

Think of each word individually as you are saying this over and over. Concentrate on the words until you feel that you *know* that word and what it means to you in that sentence. The more you time you spend doing this, the more charge you will put into it, just like in the group exercise. The technique is about getting the energy to change, and energy changes when thoughts and intentions are focused.

My Energy Transfer Story

When my last book, *Move Your Stuff, Change Your Life*, was about to hit the stands, I began to panic. I was very unsure of how the book was going to be received, because it was written in an off-beat, funny style. I began to feel embarrassed by how much personal information I had included. "Did I really put in a feng shui book that I was flat-chested and that I hosted body-painting parties?" Needless to say, I was freaking out, fearful, and a bunch of other low-vibrating emotions. I wasn't so sure I was entirely capable of handling the book's success. After all, up until that point, I had been merely a landscape architect who successfully used feng shui in my design practice, and a local feng shui consultant who did private consultations in my immediate neighborhood—not a successful writer/author.

Oh sure, it was possible that I could handle the success of my book. "Anything is possible," I thought. And certainly I *deserved* to handle the success of my book, but was I capable of it? That one didn't feel true. What does "handling book success" entail? I didn't know!

So I called in three girlfriends for an Energy Transfer. We took turns zapping each other to unblock our individual weaknesses, one at a time. (It really does make for a fun "chickfest," as I call it! Yes, dudes can do it as well.)

The next day, literally, I was invited by a television producer to appear in a segment on their show. I answered the phone, spoke professionally and succinctly, and gave him the names of the people he needed to contact. Then I hung up the phone and immediately turned around and looked over my shoulder—to see who had "handled" that call!

But it was me. I completely handled it all by myself! I was capable—yeah! I laughed at my reaction of turning around and immediately knew that the Energy Transfer had worked. I didn't have to "learn how" to handle anything: it was already a part of my energy field.

Chapter 3: Enhance Your Environment

It's challenging to thrust your new life forward if you are victimized by an egregious environment. Can you eat dinner while submerged in a pool of water? Can you breathe in outer space? The answer is actually yes, with specific adjustments to your physical environment.

The following Environment Enhancers are about making the proper adjustments to your living and work places so that they allow you to not only follow your dreams, but also arrive "in the present moment" by living out your dream-filled life. Once you properly organize, arrange, and maintain your living and work spaces, they will in return take care of you. Once you begin to enhance with these "rules," your life will literally open up to the fulfillment of all sorts of fruitful opportunities—spiritual, financial, creative, and so on. If you *feel* like you live luxuriously, and you believe you deserve it, other luxurious energies will be attracted to you. Isn't that worth a little sweeping, decluttering, and furniture re-arranging? Your mind, your body, your spirit, and your physical environment will dance with delight once they are aligned with your ultimate life and cross-supporting each other. This state will truly be heaven on earth.

Honor yourself by honoring the part of the grand universe that has been entrusted to you. It is a sacred honor to be in charge of three-dimensional space in the universe—so be wise with it!

The Yin and Yang Enhancer

You want the entirety of your home to thrive with good energy. If there's something not-quite-right about a room, there's a potential for you to end up with something not-quite-right in your life. Looking at your environment with your "yin and yang eyes" can often unlock clues as to what changes would bring balance to it.

Back in the "Where You Are Now" section of Chapter 1, you were asked to jot down all the places in your home that bugged you for some reason or another. With those specific places in mind, see if using this space-shifting technique can remove at least some of those problem areas from the list. This technique is helpful because it often sheds light on why particular rooms or spaces are not used or don't feel quite right, if it isn't obvious.

The concept of "yin and yang" originates in ancient Chinese philosophy and metaphysics. It describes the two primal, opposing, and yet complementary forces found in all things—which is really a discussion of "the one thing" we call energy. The ancient Chinese symbol that illustrates the "yin/yang" concept is this:

Traditional Yin/Yang Symbol
Figure 4

The mostly white portion, being brighter, is the "yang" portion, and the mostly dark portion is "yin." Each, however, contains the seed of its opposite, reflecting the fact that energy is an ever-changing dance between the two, rather than a static concept.

Here's a list of quick tidbits that may help you get the true flavor of yin and yang:

- Yin and yang are considered complementary opposites. They are like the two ends of the arc of a pendulum. If you were to put some descriptors or adjectives on this arc, the descriptions would look something like this:

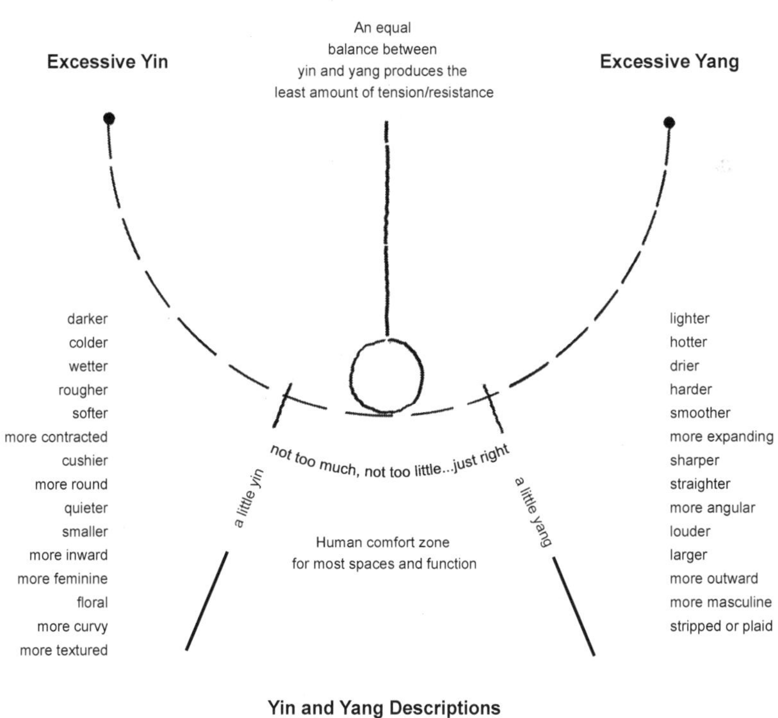

Yin and Yang Descriptions
Figure 5

- Yin qualities are usually darker, colder, wetter, rougher, softer, cushier, quieter, more contracted, smaller, more inward, more receptive, more feminine, floral, rounder, or more curved.

- In comparison to the yin qualities listed above, yang qualities are typically lighter, hotter, dryer, smoother, harder, sharper, louder, more expansive, larger, more outward-moving and dispersing, more assertive, more masculine, striped or plaid, and straighter or more angular.
- Nothing is completely yin or completely yang. All matter and phenomena, visible or invisible, are permeated with both yin and yang qualities. Even the traditional feng shui shifting techniques (or "cures") you will be using ahead have both yin and yang aspects. The yang component is the physical, visible change you create, while the yin component includes the thoughts, intentions, and visualizations that support your reason for making the change.
- Yin and yang are interdependent. One cannot exist without the other. Cold cannot exist without hot. Day cannot exist without night. In order to understand these concepts, we must understand their opposites. The discussion of yin and yang is a conversation involving relativity.
- Yin attracts yang, and yang attracts yin.
- Yin and yang qualities are in a constant state of change, always transforming into one another, just as the night turns into day, or winter turns into summer.
- Yin and yang are also in a dynamic relationship. As one increases, the other decreases. Imbalances can be described as excess yin, excess yang, deficient yin, or deficient yang.

Achieving Balance

Before we move on, you can see that the lists above included the words *masculine* and *feminine*. Of course those words are included—practically every adjective would fit somewhere on the spectrum of "yin" or "yang." But that doesn't mean that because you happen to be a male or female, your space needs to TOTALLY reflect that. Every male and every female has the opposing force within him or her, too. According to the rules of yin and yang, you can't avoid the opposing force, and you wouldn't want to. You're looking for balance in your surroundings to feel balanced in life, as this brings about optimal outcomes.

My client Bren lived like a mountain man, complete with a log cabin-type house filled with browns, plaids, and rough-hewn wooden furnishings. It could have screamed over-the-top "Dudeville," but he had it balanced with multiple pieces of art depicting Native American women. There were paintings, sculptures, and carvings of these gals galore. Now, we'll be getting into symbolism a little later on, but from a yin and yang standpoint, that place felt like it had quite the feminine touch even in all its brown manliness! And it didn't take long to notice that Bren had quite a nicely developed feminine side to him. Getting in touch with his feminine side was not why he hired me. He was calm, caring, and gentle in his demeanor. He definitely reflected a balanced sense of masculine and feminine qualities, just like his home did.

Yin . . . or Yang?

When deciding whether an element is yin or yang, you must consider the entirety of the surroundings. In other words, whether something reads as "yin" or "yang" totally depends on what is around it.

For example, imagine that you have a 4-watt little night-light bulb switched on right next to a shining 60-watt bulb. According to the yin and yang rules, the 4-watt bulb must be the yin item, and the 60-watt bulb must be the yang item. The 60-watt bulb is burning brighter, is bigger, and is putting out more light than the little 4-watt bulb, so the 60-watt bulb is more yang and the 4-watt bulb is more yin. Now, imagine adding a 200-watt giant spotlight into the mix. It far outshines the other two bulbs. It is definitely the most yang thing going on now. So, what happened to the 60-watt bulb? In relation to the 200-watt bulb, it is more yin. What was once the most yang thing around has now become more yin, because something else has been introduced into the environment.

This is how you are going to shift your spaces based on a consideration of yin and yang. There is no specific solution, because the shift totally depends on what is already in the space. The lightest brown in Bren's very dark brown cabin would be a very yang color *in his place*, for instance, but I'll bet it would be very dark and yin in many other places.

Practice Exercise

Here's a practice exercise to help you get into the swing of balancing yin and yang. I'll describe two client bedrooms, and you figure out which one is more yin and which one is more yang. Imagine how these two bedroom spaces feel, and think about what changes could make them feel more balanced using the concepts of yin and yang.

Sasha's bedroom is in the top-floor loft space of a converted warehouse, with 16-foot ceilings, white walls, exposed steel trusses, skylights, and a concrete slab floor with no rugs. One whole wall is a glass window, with no window treatment, looking out over a downtown skyline. Her furnishings include a shiny chrome bed with white satin bedding, a plastic chair, a square metal night stand on wheels, and an industrial-looking lamp with an exposed bulb. The art includes a metal sculpture.

Brenda's bedroom is an 8-by-10 foot partially subterranean room, with 8-foot high ceilings. The flooring is wall-to-wall shag carpeting. The bed has a dark purple, velvet-upholstered headboard with matching bedding. The curtains of the small window that open onto a light well are also velvet. Seven chenille throw pillows in the same fabric as the nearby overstuffed chair adorn the bed. The night stand is a simple round table with fabric draped over it. A small lamp with a tasseled and beaded shade sits atop the night stand. The art is a nubby tapestry.

Can you imagine the "feel" of these two rooms? The loft feels big, loud, exposed, hard, bright, and echo-y—clearly on the yang side of things. And, relative to the loft, the cushy, dark, velvety, purple room is the more yin one.

Can you imagine what Sasha and Brenda are like just by looking at their rooms? If what's going on in your environment is also going on in your life, these two people should be very different. It would be safe to guess that Brenda in the small, yin room is more quiet and withdrawn than Sasha in the yang loft, if they both spend a lot of time at home.

For practice, do a little mental yin and yang swapping on these two rooms and see if you can bring about a little more balance. Here's a start. Say the loft now has wall-to-wall shag carpeting, and the small room has wooden floors. Just that change alone drastically shifts the "attitude" of the rooms. The loft feels a bit more cozy, and the small room has a bit of breathing space.

You see, the balancing answers are going to have to come from you. If you can't figure out what to do in a room that just doesn't feel right, first try to come up with adjectives to describe it. Then try to replace, remove, change, or exchange something that would make your description more toward the opposing yin or yang side. If the room is too dark, try changing the window treatment, light bulb wattage, or wall color to add more light. If it's too echo-y, add more upholstery or fabrics, and so on. The more you practice, the easier it will be to think up quick changes. Quite often, your first gut instinct is a great start. Yin and yang changes can be grand or subtle, but either way they can profoundly affect your energy—which in turn can change your life.

The Opportunity Knocking Enhancer

It takes energy to swim in the flow of life and be a beneficial presence in the universe. So, how do you get this energy stuff, and where do you put it once you acquire some? You are going to use your home to gather, store, and "spend" energy. First, let's gather it by inviting it into the home like a treasured guest—welcoming it in through the front door.

Getting energy to your front door is equal to preparing for opportunities in life. Just as your body relies on energy from food, water, and air that enters through your mouth, a room or whole home relies on receiving "nourishment" via energy entering through the front door. This is the opening through which you'll be "capturing" the energy that will be supporting your dreams.

If you were to follow the "what's closest to you has the most impact" rule, you would look first at the door to each room, and then work your way out by reviewing the door to your whole home or apartment. But I consider the home's actual front door to be more important than the doors of individual rooms, and I would guess most feng shui consultants would do the same. The bottom line is, without energy entering the whole home, your perfectly organized, decorated, and de-cluttered room will have nothing to hold.

Front Door Cures

Because you may have more than one door into your home, it is important to clarify or intend that one door be your "main mouth." Your home's front door—or to be more specific, your home's *architecturally intended* front door—is usually the main mouth of your home's body. It is the door at which the UPS and FedEx delivery people, trick-or-treaters, or strangers would most likely knock—as opposed to, say, the door you or your close friends use because it's the most convenient door to access from the car. If first-time visitors can't find your door, or if they knock on a door that is not what you consider to be your front door, you have work to do.

> **Architecturally Intended Front Door:** *The door that the architect planned as the front door. If the architect was a good one, the door usually has "hints" near it that non-verbally communicate that it is the front door, like a special porch overhang, doorbell, porch light, mailbox, or address right next to it. It is the door that is designed for guests, deliveries, trick-or-treaters, and opportunities to enter.*

If I go to a home and I can't figure out where the front door is, I know from the outset that the occupants are not receiving all of their available energy. If I am drawn to "choose" the walkway that takes me to the garbage-can side of the home rather than the front-door side, I'd say they are getting only about half the energy they could.

If your front door is not emitting the "Hey, over here! I'm the front door!" vibe, shift it by introducing items that subconsciously say "front" or "main" door. A gate or an archway, a welcome mat, a solid walkway versus a path made of stepping stones, or simply a wider walkway than others nearby all give clues that you are on the right path to the front door. If you have several doors that a visitor could choose, downplay the others as strongly as you highlight the correct choice. Use better lighting, brighter colors, pots filled with flowers, colorful flags and mats, or wreaths on or near the front door.

Doors to Individual Rooms

Let's say that you're working on doors inside now, and you have a room that has more than one door. I'd suggest making the "front door" of that room be the door that people would most likely walk through first if they were coming from the front door of the house. (This tip will also be handy up ahead, when you are organizing the things inside each room based upon the location of the "main door." So don't forget it!) If necessary, use Enhancers to make clear that this door is the main door into the room.

Inviting Energy to the Door

Take the time to check out your front door and the doors to rooms that you hang out in the most. Don't be surprised if you discover a metaphor. If a door is blocked or can't open all the way, you can bet that your full range of opportunities is not getting in and to you, and you feel blocked or stuck in some part of your life. Perhaps a door needs a doorstop because it is not balanced on its hinges. Is there an imbalance in your life?

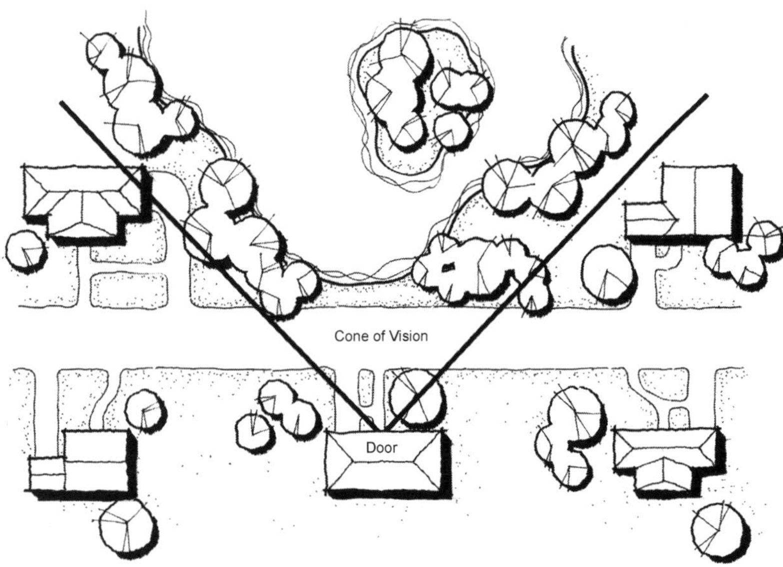

Cone of Vision
Figure 6

After focusing on getting to the door, look at what the energy must pass along the way to get to it. Focus mainly on what's in the "cone of vision" directly outside the front door. To find the cone, imagine lines running out at a 45-degree angle from your door on both sides. This is the "funnel" that the energy is directed through before it gets inside your home.

Stand in your doorway and look out. What do you see? What is your potential energy traveling through to get to your house's mouth? Is your house at the end of a "T" intersection, or on a busy street? Then you've got fairly hard and fast energy hitting you "in the mouth." How about a junk yard, cemetery, or swampy ditch? That's the skanky stuff. Do you have a fresh water lake, a wooded landscape, or a suburban street in front? Not bad at all. How about a reflective urban building taller than yours in your cone of vision? It's probably overpowering you by taking in all the local energy. What's around your home and right outside your front door impacts you greatly. These elements are in your "sphere of influence."

Feng shui cure time! If you do have something that you consider negative directly in line with your front door, deflect it away with a mirror—in this case, one about four to six inches in diameter. Hang the mirror *above* the door facing out toward the item in question, with the intention of deflecting that item away.

If you think it looks too strange to see a mirror above your door, hang the mirror inside your home above the door, still facing out with the same intention. (You would see the back of the mirror inside your home.)

Or to be even less obvious than that, get a shiny brass knocker and attach it to the door, or place a "gazing globe"/"mirrored ball" in the landscape with reflecting intentions. They can both act as a convex mirror and do the job. In a pinch, I have even stuck a mirror in the dirt of a planted pot by the door and faced it out and away from the house. Feel free to get creative!

Place a mirror inside or outside the home above door facing the energy obstruction. Intend that the mirror deflect the obstruction away from doorway.

Energy Obstruction Cure

Figure 7

Here are some more energy-gathering tips:

1. Sweep or clean the path a visitor would take from the street to your architecturally intended front door. Even if you commonly use the garage or another door to enter your house, the focus needs to be on the real front door. Make it a very comfortable path to navigate, free from tripping hazards and overgrown foliage. If your "welcome mat" is tired, dirty, or otherwise "not welcoming," replace it with a mat that is welcoming.
2. If the door to your house is not visible from the street, hang a wind chime outside on the side of the door closest to the knob to give visitors and energy an "audio clue" as to where

your door is located. If you have an interior front door, as in an apartment building, do your best to create a very cheerful door, or the "most enlivened" door in the hallway—staying within the rules of the apartment building, of course! If nothing is allowed outside of or on your door, then create a monthly ritual of cleaning it with the intention of attracting auspicious energies your way. You might want to create a reminder in your online calendar, or jot a note to yourself on a calendar to be sure to remember. (Energy follows thoughts!)

3. If there is any confusion as to which door is the "front door," use clues at the door to confirm "this is the right door" to guests. Clues can include things like a doorbell, light, welcome mat, flowers, or address sign. Avoid having these types of markers at the other doors in ways that might make them compete with the front door.
4. Clean or wash your front door, any sidelights, porch lights, door bell, and hardware.
5. Make sure that the front door opens easily and fully. If the door sticks or rubs when you open it, fix it, and remove anything that is currently stored directly behind it. Remember, what's going on in your environment is going on in your life, so if your door sticks, you might feel like "I'm stuck in life," or "I get passed up for fun opportunities."
6. If you are suffering from a health issue or have been extremely challenged in finding work while living in this home, and you do not have a solid pathway from the street to the front door, you may consider creating a solid, fully contiguous walkway that connects the two. Your home is lacking a solid pathway if you have to walk on grass, gravel, or stepping stones at some point to get from the street to the front door. Also, give friends, family, good energy, and opportunities a clear way to get from the street to the front door without having to "walk on" the *drive*way in between if possible.

The best option is to connect the street to the door with a solid pathway. It's common to have a break in this path—there may be a grass parkway between the sidewalk and the street, for instance, or your sidewalk may go from your front door to your driveway only. If you currently find yourself "cut off" from opportunities in life, bite the bullet and just get a solid pathway added. It will be the fastest way to see a big payoff later.

7. Clean or freshen up your mailbox and make sure the proper information (name, apartment number, address) is on it.
8. Speaking of addresses, here's a chance to play with the energy of numbers. Did you know that the numbers in your address give you a certain quality of energy? To find out your energy, add up the numbers of your address. If you live in an apartment, use the apartment number if you have one. If the number you get is a two-digit number, add those numbers to each other until you get a single number. For instance, an address at 555 Main Street would add up to the number 15; then add the 1 and 5 to get a 6. Then check to see what your address number's qualities are on the following list:

- **The Number 1 = Independence / New Beginnings.** That's good if you need to feel more independent in life or start a new venture, but you may feel alone even with other people around. It is a challenging address for couples and groups.
- **The Number 2 = Balance.** That's good for couples, but the challenge is that you may exclude others outside the home.
- **The Number 3 = Creativity.** This is great if your life requires creativity. The challenge is that you may feel energetically spread too thin, and your finances may be scattered.

- **The Number 4 = Security and Self-Discipline.** That's good if you have a hectic life and love to feel like "there's no place like home" when you are there. The challenge may be that you may feel like it is "all work and no play."
- **The Number 5 = Change.** If you get bored easily or hate getting into ruts, this number could be a good thing. The challenge of this number is that you may feel like life is a whirlwind or that you are making decisions too quickly.
- **The Number 6 = Service / Self-Harmony.** This number is very good for raising families and helping others. It's challenging if you already give too much of yourself, as you may give more than you have.
- **The Number 7 = Inner-Life Growth / Solitude.** This is a great number for those of you who prefer a solitary life or a life filled with inward reflection. It is challenging if you want to be social or if you value and want material wealth.
- **The Number 8 = Infinity / Leadership.** This is the easiest address for gathering prosperity and worldly goods. The challenge may be that you become selfish.
- **The Number 9 = Selflessness / Tolerance / Compassion.** This number holds energies that help the resident think more globally. The challenge is that you may be thinking so globally that you miss the needs of the individual (yourself).

Don't like your number? Change it! Use this ritual to change your address. (Consider a ritual as simply "the servant of your intentions"—there doesn't have to be anything religious about it.) Physically add a number to your address, so that when you add up all the numbers again, the sum is the number you want. But don't add the number so anyone can see it, or it might cause all kinds of delivery confusion. Instead, use the *energy* of the number along with your intentions. Use clear fingernail polish, or paint the number next to the address in the same paint color as the background surface that the address numbers are painted on or attached to. That way, you will still get your deliveries and emergency services will still find you, but on an energetic level, you'll have the energy of the number you prefer.

Storing Energy in Your Home

OK. Now that the energy is directed to the front door and the address energy is a good fit for you, it's time to gather it and store it inside so when you need some energy, you'll have it.

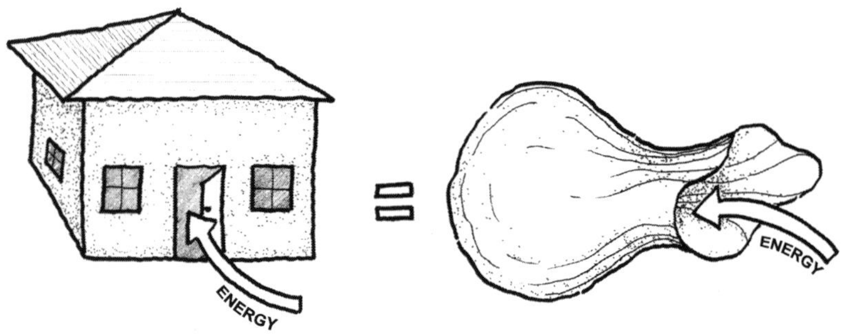

Attract, collect, and store good energy in your home like a strong sack.

Home Metaphor
Figure 8

The home should be like a strong sack, able to hold plenty of supportive, good-quality energy, so you'll be able to handle the opportunities that are sure to flow your way. The more you have of this energy, the more you'll feel supported in life and the easier life will flow for you. If your sack is empty or filled with weak, stagnant energy (think old shag carpet around the toilet), you've got to use your personal body's power and energy to try to stay in the flow.

The *quality* of the energy in your home is also definitely important. Remember, everything is made up of it. You don't just want a big bunch of the skanky kind clunking around your house. Imagine the yin and yang pendulum illustration applied to energy, and you'll better understand that there are varying degrees where the energy speed, flow, and direction feel good to us. Not too fast, not too slow—but somewhere comfortably between—is what is most beneficial.

How do you know the difference in the quality of your home's energy? Once again, check into what's going on in your life and see if there's a home environment connection. If there are places in the house that are clutter magnets, have strange odors, seem to be dirty all the time, or feel "off" somehow, you've probably got some weakness in energy quality.

When it comes to energy, think Goldilocks. You want it to feel not too fast or erratic, not too slow or still, not too wobbly or irregular, but just right. Energy that feels "too fast" usually travels in straighter lines. Think the streets of New York City (a.k.a. "the city that never sleeps"). Energy that's "too slow" is like a country road filled with tight turns to maneuver. "Wobbly or erratic" energy hangs out around protruding corners or under ceiling fans.

You want to attract energy in your door and direct it throughout your home in a nice, orderly, smooth fashion. If that's not happening, create a cure to balance out the situation. There are many ways to change the quality of energy around you. Some methods change the direction or movement of the energy, and some change the quality of it. I'm guessing you have already employed feng shui cures in your home and you don't even know it. For example, perhaps you've added a light in a corner of a room that always seemed somber or gloomy. That's a cure! You've changed the quality of energy in that space. Or maybe you "baby-proofed" sharp corners of a coffee table by putting rubber bumpers on them—that's a cure!

Oh, and by the way, just as the hidden clutter in your drawers still affects your life, a hidden feng shui cure will do the same thing. You don't have to be obvious in the name of feng shui unless you want to be.

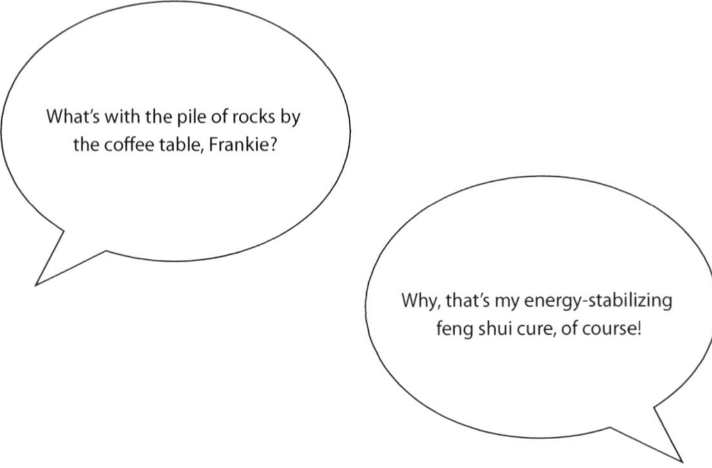

If you can figure out how to do it, you can hide your cures and they will still work!

Try a few of these energy enhancing ideas and see if you can quickly get an unexpected opportunity to show up. That way you'll know you are plugged in to a good energy source!

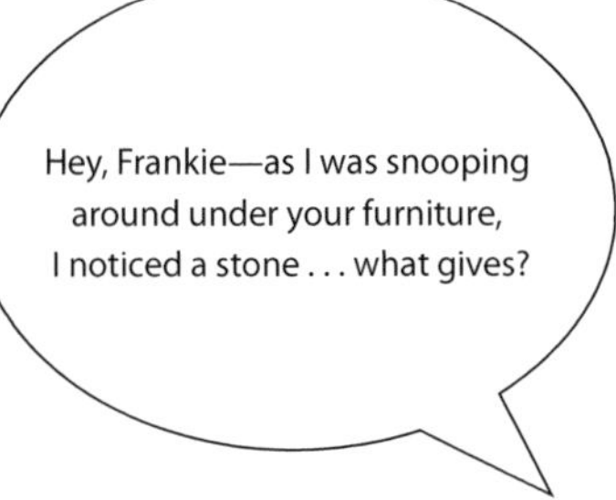

> The physical part of your cure does not have to be seen to work. Just as your hidden clutter affects you even when out of sight, a hidden cure will change the energy and uplift you even when unseen.

The Space Equals Opportunity Enhancer

Space equals opportunity. In case you sped past that last sentence, let me repeat: SPACE EQUALS OPPORTUNITY! Fully understanding and living by this three-word credo can massively shift your life. Having an appropriate amount of space will lead you to generate opportunities. With opportunities and choice come an empowered life!

> Any object that is in your space that is not cherished, needed, or used is taking up the very space that could be receiving new opportunities, prosperity, good relationships, health, fulfilling career choices, and items that can actually support your Dream Outcome.

When it comes to clutter, a good rule of thumb is that you need *at least* as much space as you have stuff. The minute you surpass the 50% stuff-to-space ratio, you start slowing down your energy, lessening opportunities in life, and stopping the optimal amount of money, love, and general good health from flowing toward you. In other words, you've built a road block in front of the candy store, and as much as you need a sweet fix, all you can do is window shop.

Although many people make clutter-clearing more difficult than it is (refer to the Mind Modernizers, please!), an opportunity-filled life "in the flow" is one where you would simply:

1. Notice an object in your environment;
2. Remember the Dream Life that you wrote down in the beginning of this book and decide if the item supports or detracts from that life; and
3. Remove the item if it detracts, repair it if is a part of your Dream Life but is damaged, and leave it just where it is if it is indeed working for you now and is necessary in that Dream

Future. If you are confused, literally stop and ask yourself, "Do I want this item more than the Dream Future that I wrote down?" (That ought to flush out any questions as to whether the item is taking up valuable "opportunity space.")

The 50% Test

Can you see the connection between space and clutter and what's going on in your life? Clutter is *anything* in your environment that is not used, is not loved, has not moved one speck in at least two years, or, like I said, fills a space more than 50% full. I also define clutter as having more than 50% stuff to space—period. You have to think 3-D here. It's not like I want to physically see half of the bottom of every drawer in your dresser. I'm talking about the top half of the volume of drawer space, so there is enough room to move things around and easily see what's in the drawer. In other words, spring-loaded sock balls jumping out of the stuffed drawer as you open it are on the "no-no list."

Likewise, there's no need to see half of the clothes rod in the closet empty either. Instead, have a quarter or half an inch between each hanger instead of all the hangers jumbled up and crossing over each other on the rod.

Can you pass the 50% test? That's 50% of your wall space (oh yeah, I've seen walls so packed with photos, montages, and posters, it would make your head spin!), 50% of the mantel top, and 50% of the bookshelf space left open. (For bookshelves, pull all the books forward, flush with the front edge of the shelf. The "space" is actually behind the books. And there's a bonus: you can't display little knickknacks in front of the books anymore—yeah!)

And let's not forget the invisible and e-clutter. Noise can be considered clutter in a space. Packed hard drives and filled email inboxes can also create stifling energy conditions. If you are starting to hyperventilate while reading this, or if you have the "I can't even see the possibility of ever getting out from under my clutter, so what's the point of trying?" attitude, take a breath and try the next technique.

A Pre-Clearing Technique for Those Who Have Surrendered to Their Clutter

Are you sitting in your home thinking to yourself, "Yeah, I'd like to de-clutter, but it's hopeless. I'll never get through it all, so why start?" If this is you, take note.

Get a pack of post-it notes. Let each post-it note represent one increment of time that you decide is the "threshold" amount of time you will give to one clutter-clearing session. Perhaps each post-it note equals five minutes, or perhaps each equals one eight-hour day. The amount of time is whatever you decide you are able to do.

Next, go around and place a post-it note (or several post-it notes) on each pile or area of your space that needs help conforming to the 50% rule. Now, count up the notes. You can see that there *is* a light at the end of the tunnel, and there *is* a calculable length of time that it will take you to become clutter free. Perhaps you have 60 post-it notes around your home. Then you know that if you do one "noted" pile or area a day, it will take you two months to be clutter free. To get yourself started, *clear some space* in your schedule to de-clutter—doing one will help create the possibility for the other. Maybe you also need positive reinforcement. Begin by removing clutter from a single room or even a drawer and see how you feel afterwards.

It's not "hopeless." It can be done given enough time and commitment. (Remember, Providence will intervene with commitment!) Maybe your newfound commitment will attract a new friend who loves to clutter-clear!

Beth's Story

If you're stuck here, and are so locked up that this technique does not even seem like a possibility—or if you feel that your clutter buttons are being pushed into overdrive—then take a deep breath and rest for a moment. You simply have some belief, or big story, wrapped around this stuff. Remember what I said in the beginning: *what's going on in your home is going on in your life*? Well honey, here it is! You've got "stuff." Issues. Stuck-ness. Don't beat yourself up about it. It is just more erroneous "environmental conditioning" that you picked up somewhere. You may need to just pause right now and de-bug your belief system by journaling in your notebook or doing the Energy Transfer Modernizer, and then come back here to de-clutter. If so, don't fret—you'll get there eventually.

My client Beth was so cluttered up, we spent an entire consultation of about three-and-a-half hours talking about the possibility of cleaning off her dining room table. She and her husband were empty nesters, and they managed to do anything to stay out of their overwhelmingly messy home. He spent long hours at work, and she headed up every charity event in town to keep herself busy. Beth wanted to get rid of some of the clutter, and she knew how great it would look if she did, but she just couldn't begin the process.

After three hours of me digging around in her thoughts and beliefs, she coughed up—or actually, it literally looked like she threw up—the word *revenge*. It was like an exorcism. That word unearthed itself from somewhere way down deep. She said that when the family first moved into the house, she had wanted to turn the little galley kitchen into a big family-style kitchen. But her husband held the purse strings and simply said "no." So, for the next 30 years or so, Beth had subconsciously made the house the most uninhabitable place on Earth—and she didn't even know she was doing it. She believed that she had been voiceless in the renovation decision, so she had taken control of what she could. And believe me, as the clutter came, so did other problems in the entire family's life. On top of the lack of intimacy with her husband and her weakened self-esteem, there was even drug abuse and a suicide by one of Beth's children.

The exorcism of that word *revenge* was the key that unlocked the possibility of change and allowed her to begin. She clutter-cleared that thought, and the energy shifted. She changed her mind first, and things started moving toward a better life. We did the Energy Transfer

Modernizer to help with this. She decided that it was possible for her to clutter-clear and live in a beautiful and organized home now; that she was capable of clutter-clearing and living in a beautiful and organized home now; and that she totally deserved to clutter-clear and live in a beautiful and organized home now, unburdened by the weight of the past.

Beth eventually remodeled the master bedroom and bathroom of their home—even knocking a wall down and turning a neighboring bedroom into the master closet! She tricked it out with all those organizers and such. The windows of the room made it light and beautiful. And need I say, her husband actually started coming home earlier and took an interest in the remodeling himself. They were reinventing themselves as happy empty nesters by reinventing their home.

Peeling the Onion of Clutter

Be gentle with yourself as you "work through" the issues that come up when you are working through your stuff. Peel the onion in a manner that keeps you moving toward your goals; you'll be amazed when you reach a point in time where what was once something that you could not *fathom* releasing suddenly has no emotional connection with you anymore and is free to go.

That's what happened to Beth. It started with the dining room table, and at that time she couldn't even *think* that someday it would be possible to take on her deceased son's locked bedroom. When I first visited Beth's house, that room was top-to-bottom/front-to-back packed with stuff. She kept the door locked at all times. According to the first premise given in the Prepare for the Shifts chapter, if she wasn't looking at or dealing with the stuff inside the room, she hadn't yet dealt with *the stuff inside herself* about her son's death. Like Beth, if you have physical clutter that "hasn't been dealt with," you've got a good chance of having unfinished business with life issues of the same magnitude.

As you work through your clutter, you'll notice that desirable life opportunities will gather speed and head toward you. You will feel lighter, more willing to step into your dreams, and more able to be adaptable in situations. Going through the de-cluttering process *always* eventually produces life changes that bring that coveted feeling of inner happiness.

My client Sydney could not believe me when I told her that the scratched-up picture of petal-dropping flowers on her wall wasn't helping her find a new relationship after her sexless, dried-up, and dead marriage ended. Sydney had so many dried flower wreaths, tree branches, pine cones, and pieces of fruit lying around that quite frankly, that picture was the freshest thing she had going. Her place mats on the table were even made up of little dead twigs tied together with copper wire. I told her that it all had to go, based her Dream Outcome that included "a relationship with a pulse." She got the connection about the dried real stuff, but she could not see why the flower picture had to go.

It wasn't until we replaced all the dried items with fresh, living plants and colorful place mats that she noticed that the picture was indeed "dead." What was once the most alive thing in the room was now feeling the deadest. (It's that yin and yang relativity concept again.) Sydney just hadn't been able to see it at first because of the massive amount of dead stuff around the picture.

When you de-clutter, you might have the same kind of epiphany. It's just another layer of your onion.

P.S. Sydney eventually went on to create a relationship that was very much alive and pulsing with hot steamy energy! Now she's on to her next onion layer. . . .

Warm-up Exercises

With that lengthy introduction, it's now time to take the first step to having more opportunities by doing the following "warm-up" de-cluttering exercises. No time to waste. Let's get to it!

The items on this list should take no more than 10 to 15 minutes each to do.

1. Create a healthy place for food. Remove all frozen foods from the freezer. Throw away any food items that have frostbite or that no one will never eat. Clean the freezer space, and then return the useful food items to the clean freezer.
2. Repeat the above process with the refrigerator.
3. De-clutter your night stand drawer or any furniture used as a night stand adjacent to your bed.
4. De-clutter and organize your toiletries and makeup.
5. De-clutter and organize your purse and wallet.

You should feel like you can literally breathe a little better after doing these five tasks.

If you find this list too difficult to accomplish, ask for help from a supportive friend or family member. If you feel like you do not have one of those, either hire a professional or attract one energetically. If you choose to hire someone, the opportunities and benefits from following through on the previous and upcoming de-cluttering tasks should more than pay for the help. If you want to attract someone through an energetic method, use the Helpful People Box Modernizer from the last chapter, recapped below.

Center yourself and then imagine what it feels like to have all the perfect help you need. Then, write on a piece of paper, "Thank you for the perfect help for my de-cluttering process who can help me complete this task." Then, place that piece of paper in a metal box (or wrap it in aluminum foil). Place the box in the front right-hand corner of your bedroom, based on where you walk in the door.

A Clutter-Shifting Game

At this point, you've done some pre-clearing, started peeling the onion, and completed your warm-ups. Now it's time to de-clutter the "opportunity-blockers" from your spaces in earnest using a tried and true clutter-clearing game. The name of this de-clutter game is

"Eliminate, Categorize, and Organize."[1] Remember, this is all about making life easier, and about making you happier, so get excited about this process. (Feel it!) If it feels overwhelming to even think about more de-cluttering, that's a sign that you are missing out on HUGE opportunities right now. Where thoughts go, energy flows—so let yourself really get excited, because an easier and more rewarding life is in your near future!

Directions: Get five large containers and a trash can or bag. If you are taking on a big job, you can make these containers actual "zones" on the floor, in the yard, on the driveway, or in the garage, if need be. Label the containers as follows:

- Container #1—*It Belongs Here*
- Container #2—*Give Away, Sell, Recycle*
- Container #3—*It Belongs Elsewhere*
- Container #4—*Keep But Store*
- Container #5—*I Don't Know*

You are going to take EVERYTHING in the area to be de-cluttered and put it in one of these containers so that you can maintain and clean the space before returning the *It Belongs Here* stuff. That's why you've got an *It Belongs Here* box.

Pick up your first item and assign it to one of the containers or to the trash. You've got five seconds to decide where to place each item. If five seconds passes and the thing is still in your hand, place it in Container #5, the *I Don't Know* container. Clutter often collects because of our inability to make a decision about it. As you can see, the maximum time it will take to de-clutter the space simply equals the number of items times five seconds. A-HA! It is not such a big job after all, if you did that post-it note exercise!

Container #1, the *It Belongs Here* box, is for the stuff that actually belongs in the space you're de-cluttering. Don't leave it so you have to reach around it while de-cluttering. Instead, it goes in this box.

When deciding if something truly belongs in the space, ask yourself whether you use it now and it is convenient that it is here, and whether it supports your Dream Life. (*News flash*: Items that stay should not have a "should" attached to them.)

Container #2 is easy: *Give Away, Sell, Recycle*. This box is used for stuff that you can easily get rid of—stuff that you are willing to sell, donate, or give away. There is usually very little or no "attachment" to it.

Container #3, *It Belongs Elsewhere*, serves to eliminate any excuses for you to leave the de-cluttering job site while you are working. This box is for items that are needed and used, but are simply in the wrong part of the house: like a drinking glass in the office or a plate in the bedroom. Instead of walking to the kitchen to put these items away in the middle of your de-cluttering session, you simply place them in this container for the moment. Then put the items where they belong after everything has been sorted.

Container #4, *Keep but Store*, is for things that you need to keep, but that don't have to be at your fingertips. This box is for stuff such as tax receipts and out-of-season holiday decor. You will eventually need as much space as stuff in all locations including storage zones to feel uncluttered, so be thinking about how much space you actually have in your home to store things. (*News flash again:* The bedroom is off limits for the type of storage mentioned above.) Stuff that's simply sitting on the floor in a room or in the hallway is also not allowed. This is the 50% rule at work: 50% of every space must be ready to receive!

OK, maybe you weren't the person who needed "the exorcism" like Beth did, but maybe you feel a little anxiety from reading this. Just go with it. Notice if there is a story that your mind is fabricating as a reason to panic. Perhaps you can unfurl this limiting belief using a Mind Modernizer right now and move on. I know this process requires total trust that de-cluttering is going to really produce something good in the end, and I'm here to tell you that it does. Please commit, even if it takes a leap of faith here. You won't regret it!

Once everything is eliminated, categorize things together that make sense. Maybe vases stored in the guest bedroom would actually be used and work better for you in the newly emptied kitchen cabinet. Really think about how you live and what makes sense, as oftentimes we get complacent with less-than-optimal arrangements.

Take the time to repair, clean, vacuum, or maintain the shelf, drawer, or closet that you just emptied. If you haven't moved a piece of furniture in years, I highly recommend pulling it out, wiping down the wall behind it, and wiping every part of the furniture as well. The payoff is BIG, I tell you! Do this especially if you feel stuck, clunky, or stagnant. If you want to get your life moving, get your stuff moving.

Step back, take a BIG deep breath, and appreciate your work. Notice how different it feels.

Now it's time to deal with the five containers and the trash. First, the trash can gets taken out (hopefully with recyclables separated). Hey, that was simple! The *Give Away, Sell, Recycle* stuff goes to a charity, friends, family, or a garage sale—and do I need to say *in a timely manner*? You want a new life fast, right? I'll give you a week, but I hope you do it faster. Pretty easy, eh?

The stuff in the *Keep But Store* container gets neatly stored in the designated storage area. Remember, everything has to conform to the 50% rule, so if you don't have the storage space, then you must choose another box for this stuff! Or, at the very least (and I'm not big on this), you rent space and it gets out of your immediate environment, since "what's closest to you impacts you the most."

The items in the *It Belongs Elsewhere* container get distributed around the house where they belong, and the *It Belongs Here* stuff gets placed back in the area you just cleared out and cleaned up—strictly adhering to the 50% rule, of course.

Woo-hoo! Well done, my friend! A mini celebration jig is entirely appropriate if you feel so moved.

Letting Go

Now, before we move on, I want to explain a few reasons why people hold on to clutter:

1. **Guilt Trip:** a feeling that you would be doing something "wrong" if you went against what someone else wanted you to do. This causes you to hold onto stuff you don't really like or need. An example is when you start a collection or mention you are into something, and suddenly everyone is buying those items for you for every occasion. ("I know how much you love snow globes, honey, so here's another one!") How can you say enough is enough, or stop keeping or displaying them, without hurting their feelings?
2. **Scarcity Mindset:** a feeling that you may lose everything, so you have to hold on to things you don't need, just in case. One of my clients was an artist who couldn't pass anything on the sidewalks of New York without taking it home, because she said it could be used to make her "found object" style of public art. Unfortunately, she also had the belief that "there's no money for public art anymore." Voilà! That mindset created one stuffed-to-the-gills apartment. My favorite memory of this client was that she was single, and she had a GIANT bag of boots in the relationship and love part of her house (we'll get to this later) with a label on it that said "NOT PAIRS." Single boots that had lost their matches—how perfect was that to match her single life?
3. **Denial:** a refusal to accept and honor the reality of who you are in the moment. For example, I once had a client whose

wife had died three years before I arrived for our consultation, and I had to literally *step over a folded massage table* to get into the house. His wife had been a massage therapist, and that was where she had last left her massage table. Yes, it had been there for three years, and he had stepped over it to enter his home ever since. He didn't even notice it until I pointed it out—he was so used to it. It was as if he literally denied its existence and was waiting for his wife to come back and move it. Another possible example is someone who has many clothes in the closet that have not fit in years.

4. **Identity Crisis:** a feeling of fear or grief over the loss of self-image. My client Patsy was a good example of this. She had been a costume designer in Hollywood back in the "mink stole and tiara at the Academy Awards" days, but now she was retired and living in another city, where she was only known as "the Dog Rescue Lady who had WAY too many dogs." All her furniture, walls, and floors, were trashed by the dogs. Although it had been 40+ years since she had been a designer, Patsy still had all her crispy and yellowed paper costume patterns hanging on garment racks in her garage. One match and this place was toast. I talked to her about freeing herself of the patterns so she could make room for a new passion and career, but she just couldn't bring herself to do it, even though she said she wished she could. Long story short, we did a salt-burn Space Clearing ritual as well as some "Dream Diary"-type visioning, and believe it or not, that very night Patsy's washer hose broke and flooded her ENTIRE home with about 24 inches of water while she slept! The water ruined everything, including the patterns in the garage. She called me very excited the next day and said, "it's all ruined—I've already called the dumpster to come! I am free!"

Armed with this information regarding why you may be holding on to some of your clutter, let's move on to the *I Don't Know* box. If you've been wondering what you were going to do with the *I Don't Know* items that you have been collecting, wonder no more. There are a couple of ways to deal with these containers. My favorite one is this:

The HIDE AND NO PEEK strategy—Without opening the container, drive it to a local charity, drop it off, and make sure you pick up the tax write-off receipt. Then, drive home and create an even bigger celebration than the mini jig for all of your hard work and for all the new space you have that will surely bring new opportunities your way.

Uh . . . did I lose you? Are you still breathing? For those of you who I lost with that last strategy, how about trying this one:

The RIP OFF THE BAND-AID QUICKLY WHILE YOU AREN'T LOOKING strategy—Put the lid on the box. Give it to a friend or family member to hold for you for a while, say two to three months. (Make sure they have the space!) Or, if you have the space, tape it closed and put it in your storage area. If you're keeping it, write down in your calendar to call a friend or family member in two to three months to help you deal with this box, or tell your friend to call you if they've taken your box for you.

After the time has gone by, get together with your helper and the box. Your helper opens the box in such a way that you can't see inside. He or she asks you, "What do you *need* from this box?"

> **Need**: *Something that you would use NOW or in your Dream Life.*

Whatever you need and ask for, your helper pulls it out and gives it to you. (Just remember, you have to have space for it!)

The rest of the stuff in the box is removed by your friend. They will decide what to do with it. It's no longer your decision or problem. That's it! If you don't need and name it now, you don't see it again.

Basically, what ends up in this box are items you've been keeping because of guilt trips, scarcity mindsets, denial or identity crises. It's the stuff you have that is mirroring the negative dynamics going on in your life—who needs a big dump truck load of THAT in your house? "I might fit into it again someday." "I paid a lot of money for it." "I got it for a wedding gift." "My kid made it." "I might be able to use it for replacement parts someday." "It's the only thing I have left from my career where I was so revered." Blah, blah, blah. This stuff is obviously not in use at the moment. It is not loved. It is not needed at this time. And it's definitely not emitting "My Dream Life!" vibes.

The bottom line is this: if your life is not awesome now, you cannot afford to hang on to this stuff. It is taking up the very space that COULD be occupied by something awesome instead. You might have to strap on your big girl panties or your big boy britches to get through this task, but I'm here to tell you once again—THIS IS GOING TO MAKE SHIFT HAPPEN! I'm serious! It's the law of universal energy! I am totally confident when I say that you have no idea how fast your life will change for the better when you just get rid of the stuff that's hogging up your dream opportunity's space!

My client George asked me to weigh in on what I thought of people who have very few possessions, because that's how he would describe himself. He does yoga six times a week, volunteers his time, meditates, and is passionate about helping writers. My response was that *his life proves* that when you have a balanced physical space, you have an abundance of time to do everything you want to do! That's that opportunity stuff I'm talking about. How much time do you feel you'd have if you dismissed that giant pile of scrapbook stuff that someday you SHOULD do for the kids, or that magazine-clipping "someday I'll read" pile, or that spaghetti ball of wires that you swear, once you untangle and organize, will be really helpful with some stray project?

Oh, and here's another dream-robbing guilt ball. I have seen people who take on the entirety of another person's stuff when they die. "Just put it all in the garage and I'll weed through it," they say. But what happens right after the garage gets filled? Pneumonia or some other disease, that's what! I've seen it over and over. Their physical energy was not prepared to "take the hit" of all that stuff.

The Physical and Emotional Clutter Connection

Most people feel joy and a sense of a big burden being lifted when the de-cluttering process is complete, and they have the weight loss to prove it. But some have to go through a ton of other not-so-fun stuff to get there. I'm saying this because I know how tricky de-cluttering can be. Some people, when de-cluttering, will take that twinge in their gut or that wave of confusion as an intuitive sign to keep the stuff, or to stop de-cluttering. This is not intuition. This is just the physical and emotional connection to that stuff in your environment. You simply can't have stuff in your space without some energetic connection to it. And I'm here to tell you, the connection is often literally physical. When you get rid of stuff, you usually feel it somewhere in your body.

When my son was a few months old, we got a highchair. The whole time we used that highchair, I didn't like it. It seemed like a constant food grime collection zone. I was happy knowing that this thing was temporary. Then, when my son got a bit older, we put it in the garage one day to see if we could live without it. A couple of months went by and we decided, "yes, it can go." Yeah—garage sale time! I stuck a $5.00 tag on it and happily hauled it onto the driveway. Someone came along and bought it. Now, you'd think I'd be jumping up and down with my new five dollar bill, but no! My husband and I both got a little weird—almost misty—as we saw this thing being put into the back of a truck. I was slightly panicking inside. "Five bucks! I should have asked for ten!" I'm thinking. Sadness swept over us both. I couldn't believe what I was feeling; I hated that chair! I was not expecting anything like that to happen.

But about ten minutes after the chair went down the street and out of sight, I jumped up and down and said, "YEAH—I got five dollars for that highchair!"

That's how it *physically feels* to get something out of your energy field. It's like un-sticking yourself from something. Don't fool yourself into thinking that it's your "intuition" telling you not to get rid of an item. The twinge or confusion that you feel is just energy shifting—for the better, I might add.

Here's how clutter can also clog up mental energy. My widowed mom decided she wanted to get rid of the "big house" and move into a condo. So, she bought one pre-construction. While she was waiting for it to be finished, my brother decided to buy her house. So, he sold his. Unfortunately, he sold his before her condo was completed. Being the brother-who-doesn't-listen-to-his-feng-shui-expert-sister that he is, he proceeded to move his pregnant wife, small child, big dog, and all of his furniture into good ol' mom's house, even though her house was already quite full of her stuff from her 44 years of living there. Oh, she's neat and clean about it, but she's definitely got stuff. For some reason (that reason actually being that I live 3,000 miles away from them), my brother didn't even organize his stuff in such a way that it would be easy for mom to pick up and leave when her condo was finished. It was basically, "Scoot your stuff over—here comes our couch!"

My mom was still working as a nurse during all of this. I say this to relay to you that she was still active and independent. But a week or two after her house literally doubled with stuff, I sensed stress in mom's voice. I asked her if she wanted to stay with me until she could move into her condo, but she was so confused and disoriented by the clutter intrusion that she couldn't even figure out how to book a flight, pack, and make the trip. It was like she had become a disoriented "dingbat" overnight.

What's the purpose of this story, you ask? Most people think that moving slowly, being confused, and becoming forgetful are only signs of aging. My mom's story illustrates that quite possibly, it's not the aging that is making older people "act old," but rather, it's the filling of their space that zaps them of their wits and energy. When you are young, you usually don't have much furniture and stuff to call your own, and you've got energy to burn (unless perhaps you rent a room in a totally cluttered-up house). Then you buy a house or move into an apartment, and the accumulation of stuff begins. Week by week, you nip away at your space. Week by week, you nip away at your energy—but it goes unnoticed. And then one day, the tipping point hits, and *wham*—you're a dingbat!

In mom's case, once she moved into her condo and got it organized, her fog lifted and she was back to being her perky ol' self.

So, to avoid turning yourself into a tired, confused, and slow-moving elder before your time, remember: when you bring those bags home from shopping, DON'T THROW THEM OUT! You must fill them with other stuff before they leave the house JUST TO KEEP IT ENERGETICALLY EVEN! Boxes from TV and online purchases are in the same category. Grocery bags, however, can be tossed as their contents will eventually leave the premises. Don't bog yourself down, please! I know it's a big pill to swallow, but it's a great way to ensure a long mentally and physically healthy life.

Another situation that brings up temporary "dingbat characteristics" is the home renovating process. Home renovating can be as chaotic and energy-robbing as it gets. Some of the more common "side effects" I've seen with renovating clients (or ones that start a project and don't ever get around to finishing it) are relationship strain, confusion, stress, illness, lawsuits, blown-out backs, accidents, and memory loss/forgetfulness, just to name a few. But what would you expect?

If you can't move elsewhere during a renovation, my advice is to attempt de-cluttering as fully and completely as possible before beginning the process. Then, as you proceed, choose to make specific areas top priorities for cleanliness, order, and "sanity"—to counterbalance the disorganization of having construction dust, demolition, and loud noises penetrating your home. Even if you just keep the refrigerator, your night stand, your underwear drawer, and your closet neat, it will help. It might even be worth your while to pay for a service to do the cleaning, so you can spend your usual cleaning time keeping things organized.

Physiological Conditions That Can Derail the De-Cluttering Process

Most commonly, I have seen false beliefs as the reason behind the inability to de-clutter, and I suggest you use the Energy Transfer Modernizer to help get out of it. But because I'm not there to personally hold your hand throughout this process and assess the situation, I'm going to describe two conditions where you just may need a little additional help.

On occasion, I have seen situations where it may be a person's physiology that keeps them from being able to de-clutter. *Sleep deprivation* and/or *sleep apnea* are common diagnoses. According to an article in *Sleep/Sleep Disorder News*, "Scientists already know—and most of us can confirm firsthand—that lack of sleep impairs cognitive function. Sleep-restricted individuals have a shorter attention span, impaired memory, and a longer reaction time."[2] This article also goes on to say that the part of the brain that helps you "think spatially" (as in what to do with the stuff in your space) is not able to rejuvenate itself without the proper amount of sleep. So, if you think that might be you, try getting more sleep to regenerate the part of your brain that handles organization, or visit a doctor or healer for the goal of quality sleep. (My hope, though, is that if you follow through with all the tips in this book, you will start getting a good night's sleep on your own. It's totally possible!)

The other condition is a psychological one that just may be handled more quickly if you seek professional help. There is a term coined for the total fear of clutter-clearing: "hoarding." If you can't follow through with Chapter 2's mental de-cluttering techniques, consider hoarding-targeted therapy. Find someone who is familiar and has experience with this specific condition. The right therapist can help you through the quagmire of inaccurate thoughts, so you can unlock your mental and physical clutter. It *is* possible.

After clearing out the clutter, it should literally be easier to take a bigger breath—a big bonus if you suffer from asthma or other lung ailments.

Cleaning and Repairing

Of course, this might seem like a no-brainer, but it has to be said. If you want to get on the fast track to your best life, after removing the clutter, be sure to properly clean your living spaces. If your place has been totally de-cluttered, you've probably handled most areas already. But for those still hanging out with sticky, greasy kitchen cabinets, cob web-covered garages, stinky, animal-pee-stained carpets, or haven't-been-painted-in-decades walls, now's the time to get after these. Once again, pay it forward and have the place professionally cleaned if you don't have it in you or you feel you don't have the energy or skills. That is money well spent, when you consider that it up-levels the energy for the mind, body, and spirit as well as the environment! Dust is clutter. Hair wads in the sink or in brushes are clutter. Bits of kitty litter that got away from the box are clutter. Grime is clutter. And if it is in your house, it's in YOUR LIFE. No one specifically CHOOSES to have more of these things, but they arrive under the radar. If you don't want opportunities to pass you by under the radar, handle this uninvited stuff.

I have dedicated many a word here to the subject of making way for opportunities. I cannot stress enough how this one Environmental Enhancer can profoundly shift your life for the better. Please do not disregard this information. And if you have done some de-cluttering or completely de-cluttered and cleaned your environment, congratulations on having created new opportunities for yourself!

The Space Clearing Enhancers

Ritual: *Something done as a ceremony, or something done to serve or aid your intentions.*

Now that you've de-cluttered unnecessary or detrimental physical items from your space, it's time to shift the *quality* of the invisible energies that may be holding you back.

Sometimes, there's just something icky about a space or place—even if it is clean and de-cluttered. It could be something obvious, as in odd-smelling, ugly, scary, or what have you, but it also could be something you sense that is completely outside the realm of the regular five senses.

Anytime you move into a new or different place, feel an icky vibe in your existing home or workplace, or just want a fresh start, do a space-clearing ritual to clear out negative energy that may be lurking there. Don't get freaked out about the word "ritual" by putting it in the "religious" category; I'm not using the word in that context. The term ritual simply refers to doing something physical to mirror or match your inward, invisible intentions. There are several space-clearing rituals from which to choose. If you've already got a favorite, feel free to use it. If you don't have a favorite or simply want to try something new, here are the ones I personally use.

1. **The Orange Peel and Water Ritual.** I use this one for a general energy "lift" if the space feels stagnant or lifeless, or to "top off" a space just after cleaning it. Get an orange and a bowl with fresh water in it. Peel the orange (preferably into nine pieces of orange peel) and place the peels in the water and stir. Dip your hand in the water and then walk throughout the stagnant spaces, flicking the water around. Put your thumb,

middle, and ring finger together to flick the water, avoiding fabrics and surfaces that may stain. Do this while holding intentions of clearing out any negative or stagnant energy.

2. **A Sound Ritual.** Clap your hands, play classical music, or activate a drum or singing bowl. Almost any quality sound can work to eliminate negative energy—even your voice. In the consultations I do, I usually ring my Tibetan bell. While holding my client's intentions, I activate the sound by running a wooden dowel around the bell to create a clearing tone. The bell makes a very penetrating sound that knocks any stagnant energy right out.

   Unless you've got some really nasty situation going (such as the site of a murder or other untimely death), these two techniques should work well to clear the space.

3. **Burning Salt.** My favorite ritual for BIG JOBS is to burn salt. By "big job," I mean anything my Tibetan bell can't handle, like the ones I just mentioned. But feel free to use this ritual anywhere, because it will handle whatever you throw at it.

Here's what you need and how to do it:

You need—One coffee mug (or other small, fireproof container) that you are willing to throw away, a fire-safe place to set the container, some Epsom salts, an unopened bottle of high-alcohol-content alcohol, and a match.

Directions—1. Place the mug on a brick, the fireplace hearth, or even in a shallow pan of water. (We're doing these things for fire safety.)

2. Fill your palm with the salt and place the salt in the mug. Repeat two more times.
3. Open the alcohol and pour in just enough to cover the salt. (I prefer Bacardi 151 for this ritual, but use whatever alcohol you can find. Sometimes regular rubbing alcohol does not have a high

enough percentage of alcohol to burn, which is why I suggest the Bacardi.)

4. Light a match and drop it in the mixture.
5. While the mixture is lit, visualize any negative, sluggish, or inappropriate energies going into the fire and being transformed into positive energy or simply being taken away. You can add any mantra, mudra, prayer, intention, or thought that feels right or necessary.
6. When the salt burns out, let it cool, chip the salt loose from the container, and then flush it down the toilet. Or simply throw the entire mug and all its contents into the trash outside of the home.

That's it—grubby invisible energy cleansed.

If you don't like any of these rituals, try something else. There is a wonderful book by Denise Linn called *Sacred Space* that has a ton of great space clearing methods inside.

I'd recommend taking note of any feelings or experiences you have before and after you do any of these rituals, as a way of practicing mindfulness and honing your intuitive skills. You might also want to mark this page, so you can find it easily and do these rituals throughout the course of reworking your environment and life. I like to perform these rituals after de-cluttering, if I'm feeling stuck, after someone leaves my house who has brought bad news or energy, or just to center myself and clear my head. In other words, feel free to space clear anytime!

The Proximity Enhancers

Sometimes, it's not the item in and of itself that is a feng shui or "life-optimization" problem, but the proximity of that item to something else in the environment. There are many of these potential proximity issues, but the top three spatial relationships that I always consider are where you sleep, go to the bathroom, and cook.

Long ago, before there was indoor plumbing, if you wanted to create a healthy living environment, you had to be very cautious about the location of these three particular functions in space. "We cook here, we sleep there . . . and we go poopoo WAY over there. If anyone does anything to mess with this system, you're out!" Everyone knew the importance of separating sleep, poopoo, and cook—their lives depended on it (and in underdeveloped nations, this rule still applies).

Flash forward to homes these days, and you can see how this rule has pretty much been tossed right out the window. Sometimes, there are bathrooms inside bedrooms, and toilets literally on the other side of the six-inch wide wall from the stove or the headboard of the bed.

Also, if you look at your floor plans or consider multiple-story homes or high-rises, sometimes "poopoo" (the toilet) has been placed directly above "cook" (the stove) or "sleep" (the bed). Sometimes the giant spa bathtub is directly above the bed or stove too, which is certainly a spatial arrangement to ponder: sleeping or cooking being dowsed by water, and showing up feeling like you "can't get your nose above water."

So, think 3-D in your home, and figure out if you have any odd adjacencies like this. (If you've got them, blueprints or plans of your home might be helpful.) Then apply these simple traditional feng shui cures as needed.

Common Feng Shui Cures

Along with your "invisible" intentions, there are three physical objects that can help protect you from just about any item that is weakening your power because of poor proximities. Your thoughts or intentions are what drives the success of these cures, so be very specific as to the request you are making when you use a cure, and you will see proper results. You may have already employed one if you worked the Opportunity Knocking Enhancer.

1. MIRRORS: A mirror is used to deflect things away, to double whatever it is reflecting, and to erase whatever is behind it. The job it does depends on the intention you give it. What size mirror do you need? It depends on the job. If your intuition isn't telling you anything, I would suggest starting with a mirror between four and eight inches. Then notice if you start seeing results (you'll see in a minute what I mean). If you know applied kinesiology or another divination method, you might want to apply it here to "receive an answer." Also, if you use a mirror for a feng shui cure and it breaks, that signifies it wasn't big enough to do the job (as opposed to the "seven years' bad" luck superstition).
2. CRYSTALS: A crystal—the leaded glass kind, usually round and multi-faceted—is used to break up energy lines by "sprinkling" the energy similarly to how a disco ball disperses a beam of light when it strikes the ball. If where you spend a lot of time is "in line with" something not so good, you can hang a crystal between you and the offending item to break up its energy. For example, if you walk down a long hall to enter your bedroom, and your bed is straight ahead, that's a "speeding energy" straight line that a crystal can help break up. Hang the crystal from a string or cord high enough so that it does not hit anyone on the head!
3. THE COLOR RED: Red either stops energy from crossing over it or activates energy and draws attention to it, depending on your intentions once again. The red item can be paint, ribbon, tape—whatever, as long as it is red. And by red, I mean a color in the red family that actually attracts your eye to it given its surroundings.

Armed with mirrors, crystals, and the color red alone, you can make HUGE shifts in your living spaces. Here are some quick-cure ideas for bedrooms, but feel free to extrapolate for any weak position.

1. If a toilet, stove, fireplace, or anything else energetically incongruent is on the other side of the wall from the headboard in the bedroom, face a mirror against the headboard wall. I usually just lean the mirror against the wall on the floor at the headboard. Set the intention of pushing anything inside the wall (like plumbing for a toilet) AND the item on the other side of the wall away from the bed.
2. For a bathroom above the stove, place a mirror face-up on a shelf above the stove to push the toilet away, so the stove fire is not doused. If the toilet is above the bed, perhaps place the mirror face-up on top of the headboard with intentions of pushing the toilet away.
3. For a sloping ceiling above your bed, or wherever you spend a lot of time, place a mirror somewhere between you (lying in bed) and the ceiling, with the mirror facing the ceiling. Hold the intention of deflecting the sloping ceiling away from you. Sometimes I place the mirror on a higher piece of furniture, or even at the top of the headboard.
4. When you are lying in your bed, if there is an exposed beam or tray ceiling directly above your body, hang a crystal from each offending item. Also, it would be best if these beams were painted the same color as the ceiling—preferably white. An alternative to using crystals would be to cover the beamed ceiling with fabric in such as way that it hides the sharp edges of the beams and creates a soft, billowy-type "canopy."
5. If a door to a room is in line with the bed, and you can't move the bed to get out of the harsh energy line, you can either run a line of red on the side of the bed frame that's in line with that doorway with the intention of not allowing the energy to cross the red line, or hang a crystal from the ceiling somewhere between the door and the bed. (If the door is at the foot of the bed, I'd do both, as this is considered extremely weak.)

6. If there is a "poison arrow," which is a corner of the room that juts inward toward your bed, hang a crystal from the ceiling right at the corner, to disperse the line of energy that crosses over the place where you spend time. Poison arrows can be created by the corners of furniture as well.

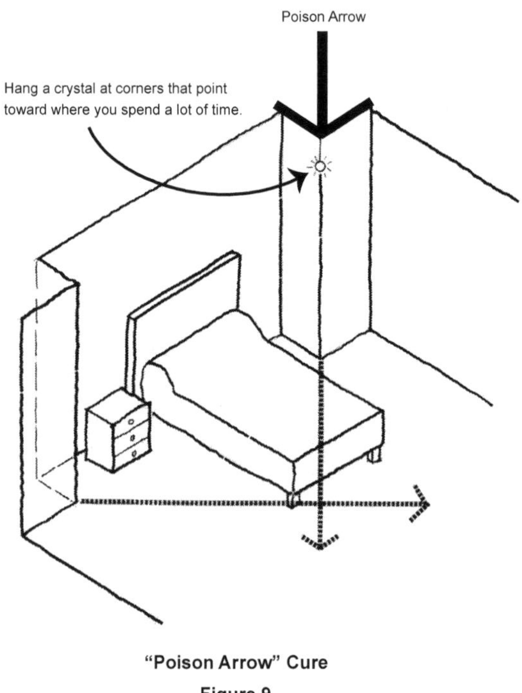

"Poison Arrow" Cure

Figure 9

7. If you have a ceiling fan above the bed or an office desk chair, hang a crystal from the fan pull to disperse the energy pressing down on you.
8. If there is a window near or above the headboard, place a strip of the color red across the window with intentions of stopping the energy from crossing over the strip. The strip

can be hidden in the window treatment or on top of the moulding. You may also use a mirror in the window facing out as well.

9. If there is a room or space near your bedroom that is incompatible with getting a good night's sleep, place a mirror on the wall, floor, or ceiling, facing toward the negative item. The room or space might be a garage, commercial space, or neighboring unit that is adjacent to, above, or below your bedroom and that has a noisy, toxic, or otherwise undesirable vibe. The incompatible thing might even be moving outside your room—a train that goes by, for example. So, if your bedroom is above a garage, place a mirror face down underneath your bed. (By the way, from now on, the *only* thing allowed under your bed is a mirror—if you need one because of this issue.)
10. When lying in your bed, if you can see yourself reflected in a mirror anywhere, this is considered a health issue from a feng shui perspective, among other things. Either remove that mirror, or cover it at night so you are not reflected while you sleep. Hanging a curtain rod and curtains from the ceiling, or from the space above your closet doors, can help to eliminate your reflection from mirrored closet doors that you can't replace.
11. If the front door and a back door are aligned, or the front door and a big window are aligned, it's like your house has diarrhea! And that's not good for gathering personal or financial energy. Hang a crystal between the two with intentions of stopping the energy from speeding through and exiting the house. Also, use this cure between a front door and a staircase if they are aligned. You can also mix and match the cures and possibly hide the color red across the step tread, back door, or back window to stop energy from escaping out of the house or rolling up or down the stairs.

12. I have effectively used a dashed red line on sub flooring in homes that were being renovated or built. Yes, the cure is hidden under the floor!

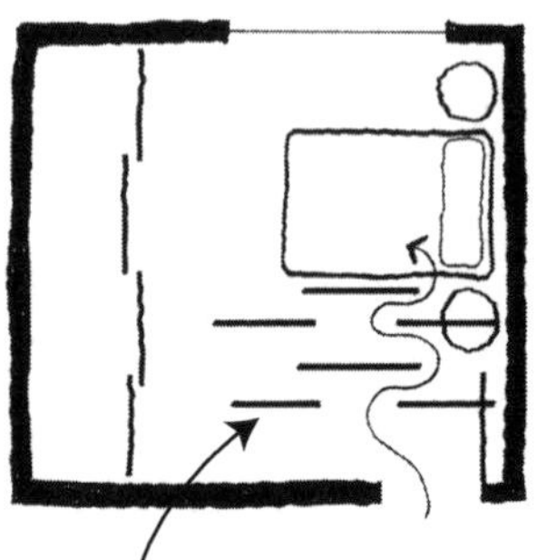

Subflooring Cure
Figure 10

There are potentially many other oddball items to cure with these three gadgets, but I think this gets the point across. Feel free to comb through your home and office for anything that you think might be working against you. If you are not sure, experiment. Cure it and see if you get results, or tweak it until you do.

The Armchair Enhancer

Story time! Sit back and relax, and let me tell you a tale about how someone figured out the optimal furniture placement in your rooms.

Thousands of years ago, in a land far, far away, a man (patriarchal world back then) built his house on the riverbank. "How lucky I am!" he exclaimed. "I have local, fresh water for my plants, my animals, and my family!" Then one day, the river rose above its banks and washed the man's house off the map. The first feng shui note ever recorded: *Move Up the Hill.* He didn't want that water to strike his home again.

So, up he went and built his house on the very top of the hill. "Oh, this will definitely do," he said. "That water will NEVER get us up here!" And it didn't. But one cold winter day, the north winds blew, and *Woosh!*—they blew his house off the map. The second feng shui note ever recorded: *Move Somewhere Between the Wind and the Water.*

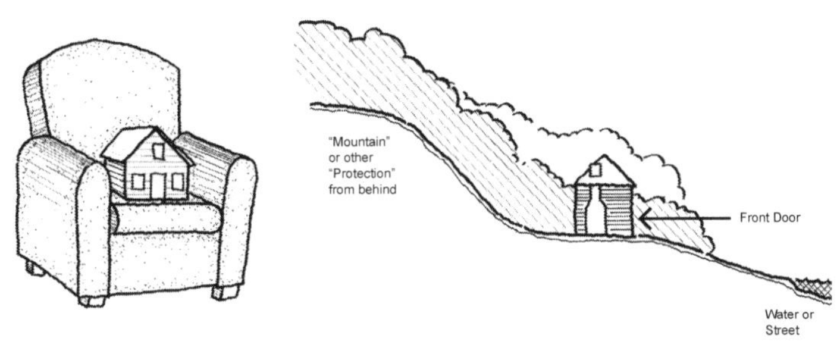

The "Armchair Position"
Figure 11

"Armchair Position" in Section
Figure 12

This tale is an example of how the wisdom of feng shui originated. The Water represents all of the "seen forces" that can wipe you off the map, and the Wind represents all of the "unseen" stuff that can do the same—like the icky vibe from the Space Clearing Enhancer, the negative thoughts and perceptions discussed in the Mind Modernizing chapter, or the radio frequencies up ahead in this chapter. Through trial and error, the man eventually figured out that the best way to be safe from both the seen and unseen forces was to build his house somewhere balanced between the wind and the water. He decided that the safest, healthiest, and most empowering place he could find for his home was halfway up the hill, with his door facing the water (or our modern day "stream" called "the street") and the hill or "mountain" at his back. It felt to him like his house was sitting in a "giant mountain armchair"—and he felt safe and protected.

Hold on! Before you hire a crane operator to come move your house up a hill somewhere, let me explain further. Remember one of our original premises: *What is closest to you impacts you the most*? Well, if your home isn't mobile, work on creating that same "armchair position" inside your home to get equally good results. Remember, it's most helpful to act on what's closest to you.

In an optimal interior feng shui setting, you want every piece of furniture—or at least the main piece of furniture—that you use most often to support you physically as well as energetically. To do so, it should give you a solid backing and a view toward the main or any nearby door, so you can see the flow of unexpected and expected people and opportunities approaching you. Your couch is usually the main piece in the living, family, and great rooms if you are arranging a public entertaining space—even if there are multiple seats in the room. The desk chair is the main piece in the office. The bed is the main piece in the bedrooms, and the stove is the kitchen's "main piece." (We'll leave toilets out of the conversation for now.)

Your feng shui power—the ability to attract, hold, and utilize the energy that supports your mind, body, and spirit—and how you can handle changes in life will definitely improve if you follow the armchair principles, especially where you spend the most time.

Something that almost immediately shows up in life when you make a move from a weak position to the armchair position is respect. Think about it. Who grabs respect? The king, the pope, the judge—all people who know the value of a high chair back (or throne back), and who usually sit in a slightly elevated armchair position. Are the peasants usually allowed to mill around the back of the throne? Can anyone in court sneak up behind the judge? No. These leaders have consistently placed themselves in a safe and empowering position. They have guards posted on either side of them acting as the "arms" of their armchair position, and they have full view of the door into the room.

If you are looking for respect, look no further. Just grab the most powerful position in the room wherever you hang out a lot, and you'll get it.

A mafia boss understands feng shui. He might not know he knows—but he knows. His life depends on it! He would never sit with his back exposed. That's like asking for a drive-by shooting in his world. He sits at his office desk and in public places in positions where no one can sneak up behind him, and where he and his body guards (his "armchair arms") can always see who's flowing into the room. No one startles the boss.

Get in touch with your inner Guido and place your BarcaLounger in the same powerful position.

Powerful Positions While Sleeping

As a feng shui consultant and healthy-lifestyle designer, I am most concerned about your bed and what is around it, because it's where you usually spend one-third of your life—about eight out of twenty-four hours. I know that if I can get you safe and empowered there, along with your office setting (another eight hours), I've got two-thirds of your life safe and empowered.

Your personal "mountain" behind you while sleeping is the headboard, and/or the wall behind the headboard of the bed. Claim a good position here, and you're well on your way. Here is my list of the best to worst headboard positions and what to do about them.

The best headboard position is up against a solid wall with no windows or doors along that wall. The people in bed have a clear view to the doorway but are not in line with it.

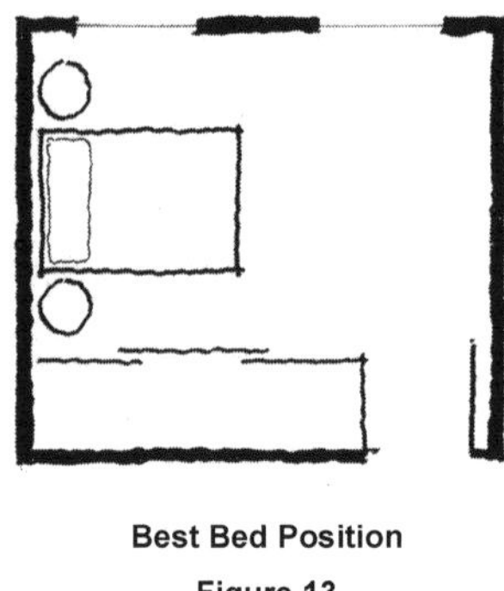

Best Bed Position

Figure 13

A slightly weaker bed position is a strong headboard up against a solid wall, with perhaps a window or windows along that headboard wall to the sides of the bed.

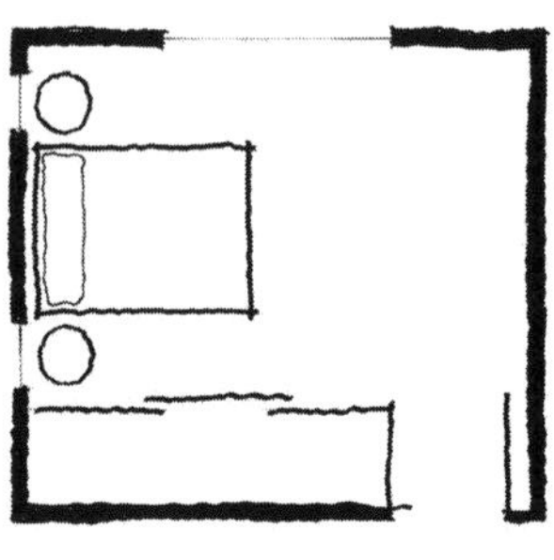

Second Best Bed Position

Figure 14

Weaker than that is a bed with its headboard up against the same wall as the bedroom door. We're officially sitting backwards in the "armchair position" here, where you cannot see who's coming into the room without sitting up and turning your head around. You have placed yourself in a vulnerable position.

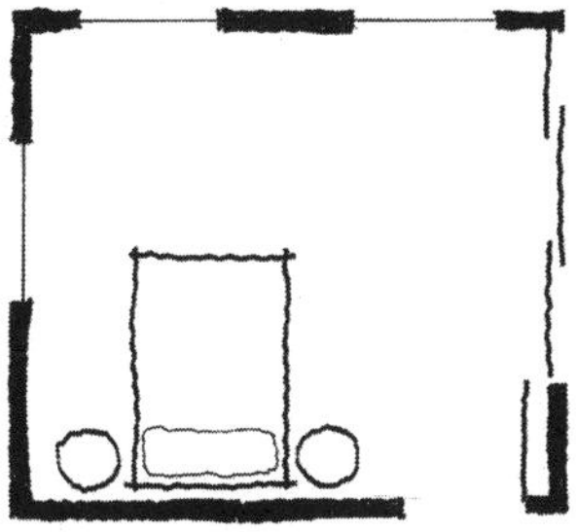

"Sitting backwards in the armchair"

Weak Bed Position
Figure 15

And weaker than that is a window directly above the headboard. Your mountain is invisible and you are definitely vulnerable and weakened by this position.

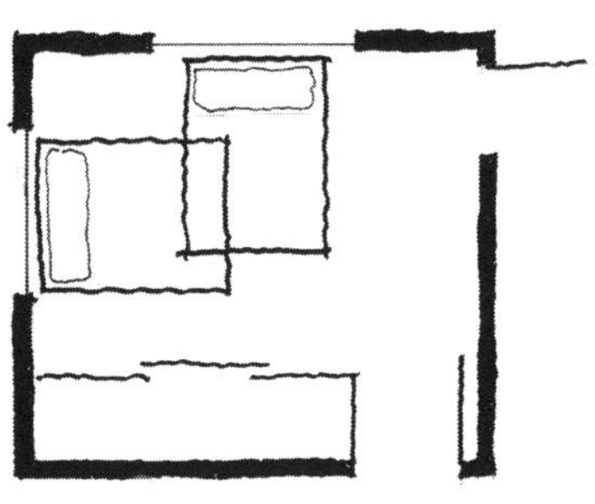

Weak "Vulnerable" Bed Positions
Figure 16

One step weaker than this actually is to have a headboard-less bed with the head zone up against a window. Yikes! Talk about a sitting duck!

And I have actually seen one scenario weaker than that. A client of mine had a headboard-less cot with its head zone up against a first floor sliding glass door! Doesn't that just sound creepy? I don't think I could sleep a wink in that position. I'd constantly be wondering if someone was standing outside, two inches away, with their nose pressed up against the door looking at me while I was sleeping. No way! Guido would never approve, and neither do I!

A headboard placed at a 45-degree angle in the corner of a room is fine, as long as it has a good armchair position with solid walls behind it in that corner. I find that a solid headboard is beneficial for beds in this 45-degree position. It keeps you from feeling exposed at your head because of the "triangle" of space created by the bed and the corner. Be sure to fill in that open space with something (a table of some sort?) to make it feel more solid at the head, if you don't have a headboard.

Weak Bed Position Cures

If you have a situation where your bed cannot be placed in a great position, cure it. If your bed is in line with the door, hang a crystal somewhere between the bed and the door to disperse the speedy energy entering the room and hitting you.

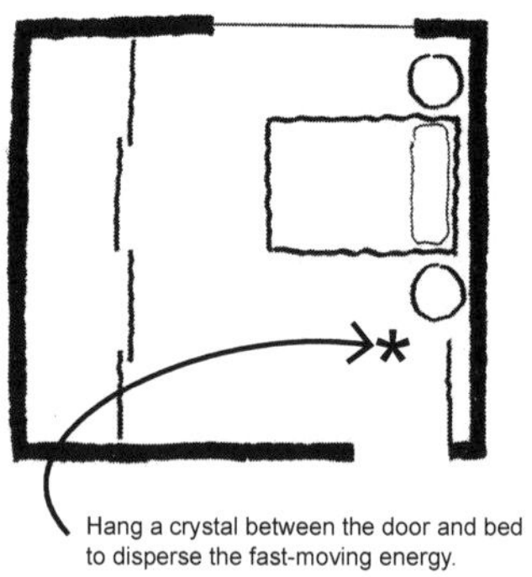

Cure for Unhealthy Bed Position

Figure 17

As I stated earlier, if you have a window at the head of your bed, you could either hang a crystal to disperse the energy, or place a line of red (tape, paint, whatever) across the window frame, moulding, or behind the curtain rod or valance with the intention of stopping the energy from crossing through the window.

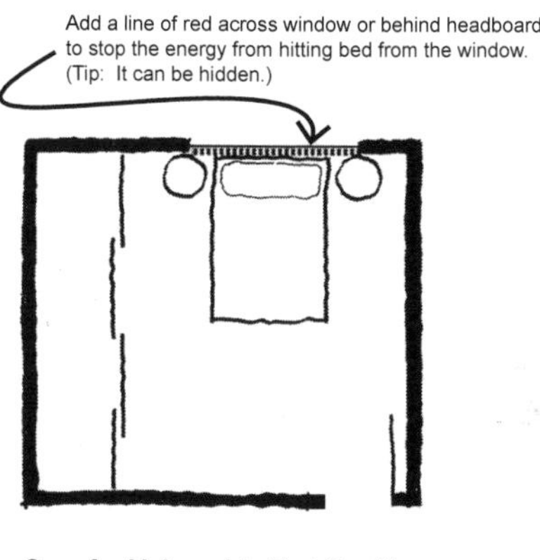

Cure for Vulnerable Bed Position

Figure 18

If your headboard is along the same wall as the bedroom door, then put yourself back in the armchair position by placing a mirror on the other side of the room from the bed, so you can see a reflection of the door in the mirror while you are lying in bed.

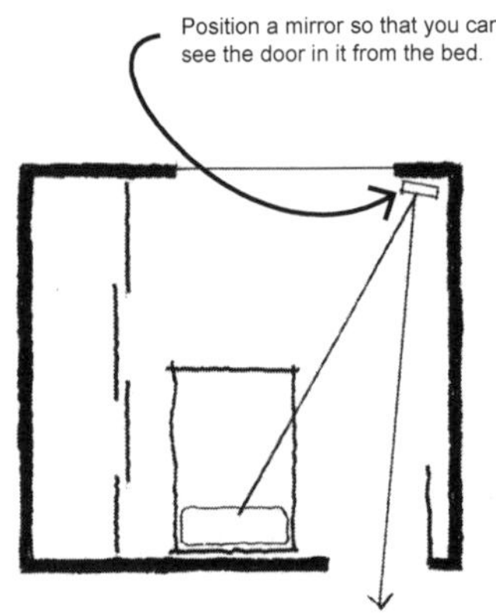

Cure for "Sitting Backwards in Armchair" Bed Position

Figure 19

Remember, what's reflected in the mirror is energetically equal to the real thing. With the mirror, you now you have "the door in front of you."

The least favorable position to put a bed is if your feet are in line with or facing the bedroom door while sleeping. In feng shui, this is called the "death position." Try choosing any one of the other positions over this one if you can. If you can't, then add a trunk, bench, or other piece of furniture at the foot of the bed for a bit more protection. Place red, soft storage items in the trunk to give you that red "energy stopping line" between the bed and the door. If you have no room for furniture at the foot of the bed, simply apply red tape along the bottom of the bed with the intention of stopping the energy from crossing the bed. Remember, you can hide cures. I'd also hang a crystal between the bed and the door for extra measure in this position.

Powerful Positions at the Office

If you spend time in an office setting, either at home or in commercial space, or even if you spend a consistent amount of time somewhere else (say, you do a hobby at your dining room table), make sure you're working in the armchair position there as well.

Once again, the goal is to be able to see the door but not be in line with it, and to have a solid wall behind you. Your chair back equates to the headboard of the bed in this situation. That big corner glass office suddenly isn't what it's cracked up to be after all now, huh? If you sit with glass windows at your back, you're using your personal energy to get the job done, because your environment isn't supporting you. The results of this position are usually at least one of four things: you *really* don't know what's going on behind the scenes, you may have people "talking behind your back," you may have physical back issues, or you really aren't respected at your job.

Here's my favorite story that illustrates this concept. Years ago, I worked as a landscape architect at a firm in Florida. Our office was on the sixth floor of a ten-story office building. The local news channel had their studio above us on the seventh floor. In their studio, they shot the news with the news anchor's backs to the windows. You could see a live view of the sun setting and planes landing behind them during the show.

One day, a couple of hair-brained guys from my office cooked up a wild prank. They got a shirt, pants, and some newspaper and pinned it all together, and they stuffed the clothes so it looked like a body. Then, they tossed this "body" off the roof of the building, so during the live broadcast, it looked like someone had just jumped off the building and flown by the window. The station was swamped with calls. But the newscasters had no idea what was going on! They hadn't seen what had happened behind their backs. From a feng shui standpoint, they were vulnerable from behind.

Needless to say, by about two weeks after that incident, a new set was built, and never again did the station use the live background for their broadcasts. They figured out quickly what a position of strength was and wasn't!

That's what you get with your back exposed—vulnerability. Not good. That's why people hate being in cubicles. They are forced into a subservient, weakened position. It is hard to command respect when people can sneak up on you and scare you from behind. They can also "talk behind your back." So, if you've got these situations going on in your life, you've probably got at least one weak seating position going on in your environment.

A couple of quick cure ideas to help here would be to place a line of red across the back of your chair, with the intention of stopping the fast doorway energy from hitting you in the back. I've even instructed my clients in cubicles to hang a red jacket or sweater over their chair back with the same intention. It looks like a solution for a chilly day, but it's really a solution for a vulnerable back!

If you face a wall, are in a cubicle, or have your back to the door, place a mirror in front of you so you can see a reflection of the door. Remember, the thing with mirrors is that what's reflected in them is energetically equal to the real thing. So now, with the mirror as a cure, you have essentially placed the door in front of you—creating the armchair position—even though you are "sitting backwards" in a cubicle.

> The more space in front of your face, the more opportunities you'll have.

The bottom line is that the more space you have in front of your face, the more opportunities you'll have in life. Even if you are not in a cubicle, you do not want to place your desk up against a wall so that the wall is right in front of your face, even if there is a window in the wall. This is still the typical, subservient, backwards, exposed, cubicle position. If that is your only option, again, cure the situation with a mirror to reflect the door and get yourself back in the armchair position—but I'd say turning around is your best option.

Let's say that you are a traveling salesperson, and although you have a desk, you rarely sit at it. I would ask you to still consider making sure that the chair is safe and empowered, because it is the "symbol," if you will, of your position in the office. Even though you're hardly ever there, the desk is still energetically communicating things about you to your clients and co-workers who might never see it.

Powerful Positions While Cooking

Since it's food energy that keeps you alive, and it's cooked at the stove, you want to be at your best while cooking. This one is a little different than the others, because it is not the actual piece of furniture that holds the position, but rather the space where you stand while cooking that needs protection from behind and a view to the door.

If the cook gets startled by someone sneaking up from behind, the startled energy is transmitted into the food, and now everyone who eats it has nervous side effects. That's a basic energy transfer—similar to when someone in a very grumpy mood interfaces with someone else, who in turn becomes grumpy.

The best position for the cook is to be able to see who is coming into the kitchen while they are cooking. If there is more than one doorway into the kitchen, the door that the cook should see is the one that people would most likely enter if they were coming from the front door of the home.

A lot of stoves are built in up against a wall, so the cook's back is to the room. If this is the case, place a mirror somewhere in front of the cook so that they can see the doorway behind them. It's a small cure, but it creates a big energy change. It's not as bad if the cooks can see who's entering the kitchen from their peripheral vision as it is when their backs are to the door.

There's one more thing to say before I conclude our conversation about the stove. The stove is considered a prosperity symbol no matter where it is in the house. The more burners you have, the more food you can cook—and the more food you can cook, the more prosperity you must have. Remember, if the stove is broken, you're broke. If it's a mess, your finances are a mess . . . what's going on with your stove is going on in your financial life, in other words. So, make sure all of the burners work well. (Even if you rent and your landlord won't pay to fix them, it would be worth your paying to fix them, right renters?) And for goodness' sake, keep your stove clean. A dirty, grimy stove makes for energetically weak food.

If you still need a little pump-up of energy in the prosperity department, add a small mirror near the stove to "double" the number of burners it has. Remember, in feng shui, energetic realities count as much as physical realities. Be sure to write down the current state of your finances now before adding the mirror to once again check in with yourself in the future.

If you are still struggling financially even though the stove is in the armchair position, it works, it's clean, and you've given it four to six weeks to see a shift, check in with what you wrote on your Personal Map to Happiness with regard to your financial success and your feelings of abundance. You may have a lingering, unresourceful belief to be modernized using techniques from Chapter 2.

OK, now . . . are you starting to catch on to how to use mirrors, crystals, and the color red to your feng shui advantage?

The Bedroom Enhancers

Now that you know the optimal "armchair" bed position, it's time to work on the rest of the bedroom, because it holds your health as well as your relationship-building energy. It is the "ground zero" room that often makes or breaks most people, so work this room as best as you can. We'll be discussing both "traditional" feng shui cures as well as what I call "contemporary" feng shui cures, which are the items that have been invented since the traditional feng shui "rules" were recorded.

Contemporary Cures

Let's start with a couple of contemporary items. As I note throughout the book, the place where you spend the most time is of most concern to me. Therefore, anything plugged in anywhere near your bed is probably a no-no. Consider this: over half of your body is made up of water. Water conducts electricity. Your body conducts electricity if given the chance to hang out in a situation where electricity is moving—and that's not good. So, with that said:

1. Test your bedroom for electromagnetic fields using a gauss meter. Electromagnetic fields are a result of "moving" electricity—as in, something is switched on. Preferably, you do not want any (as in a zero meter reading) in the space where you sleep.
2. If you can't or don't want to buy a meter to test, remove any item that requires electricity from the bedroom, or more likely, from about three feet from the bed. Whether it's a heater near the bed, a lamp on the night stand, an electric blanket, a heating pad, or a heater unit in your bed (sorry waterbed lovers), it is a no-no for health. Such ailments as fibromyalgia, arthritis, chronic fatigue syndrome, and other problems can result from being in these fields too long, say many—and my clients have definitely proven it to me. I have also seen insomnia, heart palpitations, seizures, and multiple miscarriages in my practice as well. I'm no doctor, but I've made enough house calls to connect these dots and get results with some changes to the environment. Wouldn't you want to err on the side of caution?

   If you want to heat your bed with an electric blanket, fine. Heat it and then make sure you turn it off *and unplug* the blanket before you get in, but that's about as lenient as I'm going to get. The lamps and all electrical supply cords radiate electric fields all the time, even in the off position. Unplug the lamps (or if they're on a wall switch, turn the switch off) when sleeping. Unplug any clocks on the night stand, as they also radiate magnetic fields, and their supply cords radiate electric fields. The magnetic field from the clock can reach out an average of about 24 inches, so move the clock away, or better yet, get a wind up or DC battery-powered clock.

3. Avoid placing a cordless phone or a cell phone (in any position other than completely off) on the night stand, or in your pocket for that matter. Do *not* recharge your cell phone in your bedroom at night, as the radiation pulse may cause sleep disturbances, among other things. These phones rely on radio waves instead of wires. And unfortunately, these waves and our bodies are not friends. If you need to have a phone in the bedroom, get an old fashioned, plug-in, curly-corded model (if you can still find one!) and sleep well, knowing that you've just erased an enormous amount of electro-pollution from your bedroom.

   If you can't remember the last time you slept well, try this: turn off all the electricity in the home before retiring. You may just be reacting to your electrically "hopped-up" house. (Don't worry, the food will stay cold enough in the fridge.) If you like the result, I would at least suggest installing a demand switch for the bedroom. That means that before you go to bed, you flip the switch and all the current in the walls surrounding your bedroom stops. You'll have to get a wind-up alarm clock, but the improvement in your quality of sleep might just be worth a call to your electrician! (Also, see the Sleep Balancer section of Chapter 4 for more information on how to get better sleep.)

The old fashioned, hard-wired, "land line" phones don't have a high-frequency field at all, *and* they work even when the electricity goes out!

If you are going to plug anything in to the electrical sockets of your bedroom, avoid using the plugs on the wall at the head of the bed. Run the cords away from the bed rather than behind it or under it. And no power strips under or near the bed, please!

I had a couple call me to see if there was anything I could find in their home that could be the reason why she had breast cancer and he had brain cancer. Without hesitation, I pulled out my electrical field and gauss meters, as I knew I'd find problem readings. My meter readings were off the charts. After doing a little detective work, I found the source. Just outside their bedroom, hanging on the wall, were the electrical meters and circuit panels for *the entire apartment building*. We could track the main power conduit leaving that point and coming in to feed the building under their bedroom floor.

Very few times in my practice have I suggested that my clients move, but this was one of them, because they had a situation that they "were not in charge of" to change. It's not worth the fight with the apartment manager/owner, cell phone tower owner, or nuclear power plant company—you get the idea—so in these cases, I suggest the less stressful approach of moving. This couple was renting, so they didn't have the huge financial commitment of homeowners, and they were both suffering in an extreme health crisis. Their poor bodies were getting chemo and radiation, and then coming home to rest in a completely jacked-up bed. Come on, that's not giving a body a chance.

We worked on their beliefs about being healthy and reviewed their environment for other major feng shui faux pas, but we found no greater "smoking gun" that pointed to their cancers than the high electrical radiation output.

Needless to say, these clients moved, and yes, I tested their new place before they signed the rental agreement.

4. Replace your pillow if it is over five years old with a pillow that is made from a natural/organic material that has not been treated with fire retardant. Consider this a high priority if you have ANY head issues—from sinus problems to allergies to brain tumors.
5. If it is made of non-organic material and is more than 15 years old, replace your mattress with one that is made of natural/organic fibers. Preferably, it should not require box springs or have any other metal in it. If you have a waterbed, or any type of bed that needs to be kept plugged in while you are sleeping, you would optimally replace it with a non-electricity-needing mattress made of natural fibers. Consider this a high priority if you have any auto-immune disease, multiple chemical sensitivities, cancer, arthritis, or arthritis-like diseases that include stiffness.
6. Consider replacing your bed frame if it is made of metal. Wood would be the preferred bed frame choice, ideally in a natural finish. Metal conducts electricity, and sometimes the electricity in our home "jumps" onto it, which creates a less-than-optimal sleeping situation. I have even seen cases where the electricity in the walls creates an electrical field about one foot from the headboard wall, and then this field "charges" the springs of the mattress. One of my clients with this situation was wondering why insomnia became a problem after moving into a new home. She said she just couldn't "turn her brain off" all night! Resolving this issue fixed it "overnight."

If you have a sleeping problem, or any drying of the fluids of the body (creating conditions like arthritis), "unplug" your bedroom for up to three months, and then check in with yourself to see if any ailments improve, or if you sleep better.

It definitely couldn't hurt. You might see benefits the first night. The zero-cost solution here is to sleep somewhere else outside of these fields.

7. If you have box springs under your mattress, you might have a condition where you are sleeping in a magnetized situation. Check this by taking a common compass and slowly running it down the mattress in several locations from top to bottom, to see if the compass can hold its north orientation. If the compass needle moves more than 5 degrees (sometimes they spin completely around), you've got an unwanted magnetized condition. This is a good thing to test when purchasing a new set of box springs, too, if you still want one!
8. Remove any computers, Wi-Fi hubs, or wireless devices from the bedroom. Not only are these detrimental to a good night's sleep (a.k.a. your health), but they are also not compatible with the function of a bedroom (a.k.a. your love life).
9. Remove any item that contains chemicals, kitty litter, medicines, or anything that does not fully align with and support physical health and healthy relationships. If you need some medical paraphernalia that really detracts from a "relationship-building" vibe, consider storing it out of sight—like medicine on the night stand—or changing it in some way that it is less "relationship offensive," like painting your walker or crutches in fun, happy, youthful colors.
10. Review the Ambient Energy Enhancer in the next section for any additional items that might be negatively affecting your body in your bedroom environment.

Traditional Feng Shui

Along with the contemporary cures we just discussed, here are some "traditional" feng shui solutions for the bedroom. (A couple of these were stated earlier, but I wanted you to have the full list in one spot.)

1. Optimally, your bed should not be in line with any room door. You also want the ceiling to be flat overhead. Exposed beams, ceiling fans, skylights, adjacent bathroom doors, and slanted ceilings overhead while in bed can weaken a person even in an otherwise good headboard position. If you have health issues and any of these bedroom problems, either move to another sleeping space or cure the offending energy zapper. Use a crystal to disperse the energy, a mirror to deflect it, or a line of red color to stop it from hitting you.

   As an example, place a mirror face up between your head and the sloping ceiling or beams to deflect unwanted energy away from your head. You might place the mirror on the top of the headboard, night stand, or dresser if that surface is higher than you when in bed. Hang a crystal between your bed and a bathroom or bedroom door if you can't scoot out of being in line with the door. If you must have a fan, hang a crystal from the ceiling fan pull to disperse the energy heading down upon you if the fan is directly above your body in bed.
2. Unless the occupant is a small child who tends to fall out of the bed, both sides of the bed should be away from any wall—at least 12 to 18 inches.
3. Move your bed to the position that seems most favorable considering both the armchair position and the above rules—even if it is for a while as an experiment. Four to six weeks should give you some result if you don't notice it immediately. Do your best to get in that most favorable headboard position, even if there are other "negative" things in the vicinity. You might consider changing rooms if there is another bedroom that is more suitable based on the above list. Consider all options.

> Sometimes making the changes that we resist the most can get us to our destination the fastest!

4. Optimally, your bed should have a solid headboard, with no slats or holes in it. For now, let's just say that if you are purchasing a new bed, make the headboard solid and straight across the top. If you've already got a headboard and it has slats or rungs in it, work with it for now and see if you can achieve all of your goals using the other cures and changes. I think it is doable.
5. Remove any shelves that hang above any portion of your bed to avoid head and face injuries.
6. Remove any weapons—especially sharp metal ones like knives and swords—from the bedroom to avoid surgeries and cuts. If you need to keep them in the home, preferably place them in a room where no one sleeps.

Relationship-Building Bedroom Enhancer

If you follow the above instructions in your bedroom and highly used spaces, you've done just about all you can do to support your health, so get excited! Now, if your Dream Outcome includes optimal relationships, try this list of to-do's in that bedroom of yours. They should be easier than that last list!

1. Making sure you have the space of course, add any item that would make intimacy, romance, and love bloom. This is a personal thing, so it is up to you whether you need feathers, chocolate, animal print fabrics, pink hearts, or other items to give you that sense of relationship-building energy.

Matching pairs of items work better to attract a partner that you can see eye-to-eye with than single items. Avoid the single-subject art (one flower, one boat, one girl, etc.) if you want a mate.

2. Remove any items that distract you from fully being able to enjoy the room from a relationship standpoint. Things like laundry, work stuff, workout stuff, kid's stuff, hobby stuff, meditation and prayer stuff, and so on all can be holding you back from fully expressing your relationship juju.

For some it may take a while to achieve, but if you have a plan, you'll be able to make good, supportive choices as you change your bedroom. If the cost of new furniture frightens you or seems unrealistic, do a Mind Modernizer about it. Remember, you will start seeing more opportunities in life (if you have not done so already) from all of the Mind, Body, Spirit, and Environment techniques you are implementing, so money from currently unknown sources is now a bigger possibility than ever before.

The Ambient Energy Enhancers

Now that your bedroom has been given the healthy once-over, extend your health energy-zapping search throughout your home, property, and even off-property to elevate your odds for consistent health. I mentioned the off-property search because even though that "friendly neighboring cell tower" is WAY OVER THERE, it is, unfortunately for your health, probably beaming microwaves throughout your entire home. Here's the test: If your cell phone works inside your home, it is.

It is all about building the most optimal health-sustaining environment—period. If having or maintaining great health isn't on your Dream List, go ahead and skip this Enhancer. But I'll tell you, many of my clients have found instant relief and solutions to their unsolved medical mysteries through incorporating some of the following suggestions.

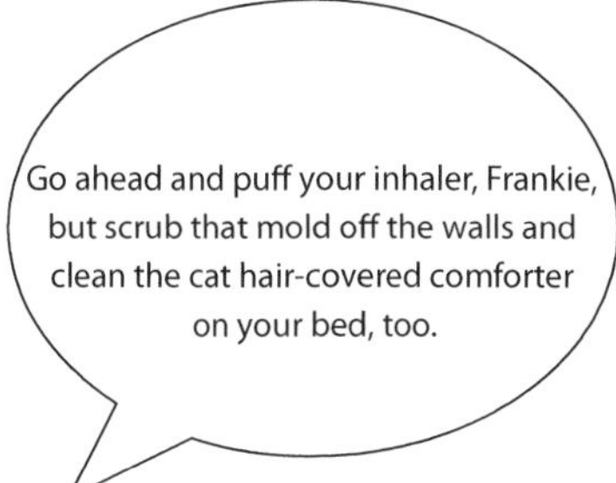

The modern feng shui consultant is much like the medical doctors of the past who made house calls. Back then, the doctor at least had *a chance* to stumble upon the physical, outer environmental trigger that caused their patient's disease.

But today, that link has been severed. Doctors see you in *their* environment. Yours is not even considered in the equation, unless your nearest neighbor is Chernobyl or Three Mile Island. Your body chemistry reacts to many things more subtle than massive radioactive matter—we just learned that in the conversation about beliefs.

Oftentimes, there are simple, zero-cost changes that can be made to create a healthier physical environment sure to encourage and allow a sick body to regain its health—especially if you can't figure out any health-robbing thoughts or beliefs.

Bau-biologie, meaning "building biology" (a term coined in Germany), is used to describe a movement promoting the use of healthy building principles as a means to improve living and work spaces and the health of people who occupy them. There are whole books and websites dedicated to this subject, so feel free to look up these terms for a more complete view of this field. I am addressing just a few key points in this section.

Electricity

It's hard to imagine living without electricity, and I don't think you have to. However, understanding how to *live* with electricity and "high frequencies" can result in a happier, healthier you.

As I stated earlier, regular electricity used in homes and offices produces both magnetic and electric fields. These together are termed electromagnetic fields (EMF). **Electric** fields are always present where there is electricity, around the wires to electrical devices and near the live wiring in the walls, floors, and ceilings. **Magnetic** fields are only present when current *flows* to power appliances and lights. There are other types of fields called **high frequency/radio** fields (RF) as well. These fields are produced by radio, TV, police, fire, and military communications; microwaves; radar; "smart" utility meters; and cell phones/tablets, cordless phones, and wireless Internet connections.

The energy levels produced by modern communication are now billions of times stronger than the naturally occurring high frequency energies from the cosmos that existed during our biological development, and they are very rapidly increasing due to the demand for wireless technology products. In a nutshell, our bodies haven't evolved as quickly as our technology-filled environments. And just because you can't see it doesn't mean it isn't there. If that theory were true, then "deadly carbon monoxide" would be an urban myth.

So, until our bodies evolve to match the output of our technology, these are my suggestions:

Similar to suggesting using sunscreen to avoid damaging exposure to UV rays, I'd suggest doing your best to avoid constant exposure to RF and EMF. Testing for these fields, and devising ways to alleviate exposure to them, has significantly added to the quality of my client's lives. If time is not on your side with regard to your health, hire a feng shui consultant, environmental consultant, dowser, or bau-biologist to test for you, or call your local electricity provider, as some companies may test your home for free. (Beware: it's hard for a company who is selling you electricity to tell you that the electrical current in your house may be harming you, so just get the readings from them.) As mentioned in the Bedroom Enhancer section, if you do have time and you're up to it, get your own electrical-field tester and EMF-detecting gauss meter and test for yourself, as these meters are readily available. If you are not into calling for help or purchasing meters, but want to do your best to protect yourself immediately, here's my best "err on the side of caution" rule of thumb advice:

Don't buy a home or live within:

- 50 miles of a nuclear power plant.
- 10 miles of a television or radio transmitter.
- 8 miles of any radar source (weather, airport, etc.) or cell phone microwave tower. (Good luck with this these days, but at least you will be aware of it and can perhaps mitigate it as much as possible.)
- 0.5 miles of a power sub-station or transmission line.

Don't sleep, work, or generally spend a vast amount of time within:

- 50 feet of a transformer can on a utility pole.
- 25 feet in front of a microwave oven that's on, if you decide to even keep it once you read up about it in the Cooking Balancer section in Chapter 4. My advice is to *remove it from your home* because it usually leaks microwave radiation, and it changes the molecular structure of the food that you are putting inside your body (which is a pretty important "environment" for your health!) to structures that some scientists say are dangerously toxic. I'm pretty sure that you would not feel at all comfortable with sticking your head in the microwave and then turning it on. Well, then why is it OK to heat something in the microwave and put it in your head (mouth)? The thing you just heated up has the same erratic, life-diminishing energy pattern now.
- 10 feet of an electrical circuit panel (a.k.a. the fuse box) or "smart meter."
- 5 feet of a television, fan, or air purifier.
- 3 feet of a regular hair blow dryer. (Oh, I'm not kidding. Get your gauss meter and test it!)

- 2.5 feet of a lamp (even in the off position) or alarm clock.
- 2 feet of any surge protector or plugged-in adaptor (*pssst!*: look down by your feet near your computer).
- 2 feet of a fluorescent light (taking into consideration what's happening on the floor above the lights, as the fields travel in all directions).
- 2 feet of a cell phone or other wireless hand-held device. WHAT? Yes, this is not a typo.

It's time for the wireless conversation. What most people don't understand is that your personal wireless devices do not work magically. They work by tossing data back and forth to each other on very small, invisible-to-the-naked-eye waves.

Our all-natural bodies exist more harmoniously if not exposed to unnatural things, and like-it-or-not, texts and conversations flying through the air on teeny waves are unnatural. If the cell tower is on your right and your hand-held is on your left, guess where that waves goes? It goes right smack dab through your body. I'm not going to get too technical here as technology changes all the time, but I would like you to—FOR YOUR HEALTH AND THAT OF YOUR KIDS AND UNBORN LINEAGE—take the time to read the fine print OF THE MANUFACTURER'S RECOMMENDATIONS on the items you use. Forget what you read on the Internet. Just read the manufacturer's recommendations. You will read that you should keep these items a certain distance from your body, which happens to be much farther than your pocket, bra, etc.

Get these devices out of your bra and pockets and away from your head! Do not charge them in your bedroom and do

Diapers that Tweet you when they're wet? What will they think of next, Frankie?

not have them in the ON position (even silent) while you are sleeping. An air-tube headpiece device is better than nothing when it comes to protecting your head from the radiation while making a call. I would advise texting over talking with the phone up against your head—as long as you do not consistently place the device in your lap or near reproductive parts or the abdomen when texting.

I'm going to get this in writing here and now, because the pendulum will swing sooner or later on this subject. I believe that someday we'll be flocking to establishments that have signs on their doors that read "Cold Spot"—like they used to say "Wi-fi Hot Spot"—because someday, we'll be searching for a place that is safe from all the high-tech energetic fallout we're creating right now. We're selling our health for immediate and constant Internet access and entertainment.

There are radio frequency-shielding paints available now if you want your home to have less microwave radiation blowing through it (assuming you aren't filling it up on the inside with wi-fi hubs and devices). There are also body-shielding products. If you suffer from major health challenges or are receiving chemo or radiation for an illness, I highly recommend looking into these products and cleaning up the invisible health-depleting nuisances in your environment. Seek professional help to create the ultimate healing place for you.

Geopathic Stress

Another invisible but potentially dangerous funk that can create health challenges is spending a large amount of time in a location that has geopathic stress, also known as simply GS. There are many other names out there for it, but for this conversation we'll just stick to GS.

Geopathic stress is a situation where the Earth emanates bio-harmful radiation. It is caused by both naturally occurring environmental conditions such as underground cavities, fault lines, and subterranean water flow, and man-made conditions like electricity transformers, pylons, building footings, and telecommunications towers.

GS is something that can occur at any time. Besides naturally occurring causes like earthquakes, a construction project a mile away may change things enough to cause GS on your property. I say this to warn you that GS is not something that you check for once in a lifetime. I'd make it a regular habit—every year or two if everyone is healthy, and more frequently if a life-threatening disease has been diagnosed.

In my opinion, the best-trained people to sniff out and mitigate GS are people who know how to dowse. Dowsers usually use their intuition, their body, and some sort of tool like a dowsing rod or a pendulum to locate invisible things such as underground water, oil, or ley lines. Dowsing takes time and practice to learn, so I would simply contact your local dowsing society to find someone qualified to come to your home, or find a feng shui consultant who knows how to dowse for GS to make sure you are free from its harmful effects.

> With knowledge comes power. Do not hopelessly throw your hands up in the air over what you might label as "bad news." It is possible, you are capable, and you deserve a healthy place to live now. Get help if you need it.

The Money and Water Enhancer

I'm sure you've heard of the phrase, "Time Is Money," but did you know that "Water Is Money" too? Yes, it turns out that, according to the premise "What's going on in your life is a direct reflection of what's going on in your mind, body, spiritual connection, and/or environment," one of the biggest tell-tale signs of abundance and prosperity (or a lack thereof) in your physical environment is the quality and quantity of water you are "in charge of." So, water, time, and money are all intertwined.

A clear, fresh-running stream is healthier and more vital than an algae-covered swamp, right? Well, in and around your home, the quality of water and how you tend to it speaks volumes with regard to your financial well-being. How would you grade your overall water quality? Do you find yourself complaining about it ("it tastes terrible," "there's always a soggy spot in the yard," "I hate the way the irrigation rusts my metal furniture and stains the walls")? It might be worth it to take a moment now to review the complaints you wrote during the Complaint Eradicator Modernizer to see if you missed any water quality connections.

To acquire time or money, you must look at the stewardship you are providing to your entire environment—but most specifically the condition of water—to see how like energy will return to you. For example, if you receive a big bonus at work and squirrel it all away (algae-covered swamp) "for a rainy day," well then, surely that rain will fall. That's a Mind Modernizer challenge! If, on the other hand, you receive and then give thanks by staying in the flow (fresh-running stream) and sharing, then your riches will abound because of the "like attracts like" flow. It is all about energy and how we perceive it. They don't call it "currency" for nothing—it's got to FLOW in the current!

Is the fountain out front rusty or dead? Is the bathroom sink drain clogged? Is the hose bib leaking? Do you squander water, and not respect money? This, among other things, could be an indicator of how you are tending to your prosperity. Running the sink the entire time you brush your teeth or taking a 45-minute shower might be unnecessary and might show up as money depletion.

So, do your wallet a favor by becoming more mindful of the quantity of water you use, the quality of water you have, and the ways you honor it.

1. Repair all leaks.
2. Scrub or clean any places intended to hold water (tubs, fountains, sinks, pools, etc.) if they appear dirty or unattended.

3. Place a circle of red (as your feng shui cure) around all outgoing pipes where water leaves your property with intentions of stopping any vital energy from escaping with the used water.
4. If necessary, add fresh water (as in a real fountain, or a photograph of freshly moving water) in a weak energy spot in your home. Classically, if you add water to the left-hand side and the left-back corner of the home (based upon entering through the front door), you will be adding to your feng shui pattern for prosperity.

Changing your thoughts about money can be a big energy-shifter. If you have ANY thoughts that it is bad, useless, evil, or anything negative, refer to the Energy Transfer Modernizer or even the Dream Diary Modernizer to help yourself get to a place where money can enter your life. When you get there, you have literally shifted the planet a little bit toward balance and wellness. I'll say "thank you" now in advance for doing this!

You can also access the "Sitting in Silence Server" up ahead in Chapter 5, if you want to feel "cheered-on" by universal energetic forces.

Woo-hoo! Turn on your prosperity hose by doing these water enhancers today!

The "If You Build It" Enhancer

A client of mine once said that before moving into her current home, she used to paint all the time. And now, she never paints. I asked her to show me her painting space, and she replied, "Oh, I don't have a 'formal space.' I just get my stuff out from under the bed and set it up when I want to paint." "Apparently you don't," I replied. Ding, ding, ding! There you have it. Having to create the space each and every time you want to do something may be what is stopping you from actually doing it.

I had another client in an efficiency apartment with a Murphy bed who eventually started falling asleep on the couch, and then eventually started sleeping on the couch full-time instead of taking the time to pull down his bed to go to sleep.

Can you relate? Is your Dream Life, or some item on it, hampered by the lack of full-time space dedicated to it? If it takes time to "build it" each time you want to do something, chances are you might not do it. For all you mobile "All-I-need-is-a-Starbucks-and-my-laptop" people who can't find a permanent job, listen up!

1. *Dedicate a full-time space to your dream.* (This is why the Helpful People Box Modernizer has a box! It is space in your environment dedicated solely to getting help in life.)

   Dedicating a full-time space is the crucial first step, but not just any space will do. One client had a full-time space set up for her home-based business but admitted she never used it. Once I saw it, I understood why. It was in a dark, creepy, unfinished basement. Nothing says "*Do Business with Me*" more than an exposed light bulb with a pull-string switch nailed to exposed floor joists above a wobbly-legged desk sitting on a dust-bunny-laden concrete floor, am I right? This conversation leads us perfectly into the next rule.
2. *The dedicated space must be pleasant enough to attract you there and comfortable enough to keep you there.* If you don't like the space, you and opportunities probably won't go near it. Enough said.
3. *The space must be appropriately sized.* Unless you had a custom house built to your Dream Life specifications, you probably never met the designer who designed your living spaces. So, unless you plan to hire one, it's up to you to think your spaces through to get them functioning appropriately for you.

   Do you feel "Lost in Space?" Perhaps you spend too much time in too big of a room. To remedy this: think YIN. Smaller, darker, quieter, curvier, earthier—all the things that define yin, because "too big" is a component of yang. Try changing things up in the more yin direction and see if you feel more grounded and "a part of."

Not interested in "intimate pursuits?" Maybe your bedroom space is too big as well. Most people feel more comfortable sharing intimate moments in more yin spaces to "show their stuff." Close the curtains, take the light bulb wattage down a notch, and add more texture to the interior fabrics, etc.

On the other hand, are you feeling overwhelmed, stuck, passed over, or like you can't do the job? Perhaps your desk or task space is too small. This is the opportunity to "yang it up" with bigger surfaces (that are obviously clutter-free and clear), more straight lines, taller ceilings, bigger views, and windows to bring in outdoor spaces.

4. *Have the supplies, materials, furnishings, storage facilities, and other elements that are needed for your dream actually there IN the space, easy to find and use.* TA-da! Simple, right? Not for many of my clients. Think "dress for the job you want, not the job you have" if you want to "build it" for a new dream on your list.

When you look at the "Where You Are Now" list that you wrote out in Chapter 1, you might have noticed that your living environment doesn't *really* have what it takes to pull the Dream Life off. A surefire way to start living that life is to incorporate the 3-D stuff and surroundings that *can* pull it off.

It would help if you spent some time visualizing the environment that would support you and note where you currently fall short. Perhaps it will take piece-by-piece building, like cutting out magazine pictures that start to give the vibe of the room you think would work for you. But rest assured, if you build it, that life circumstance will come!

Maybe the first step is actually creating the space (de-cluttering and re-arranging) to hold *at least one* component of the opportunity you wish to experience. Then, you can hone in on all the 3-D details as you build it out in your Dream Diary to finish.

How Cathie Built Her Dream

My 50-something year-old client Cathie was more than 100 pounds overweight and needed both of her knees replaced. She almost shuffled as she walked, and she clearly moved more slowly than a fit 50-something. Although Cathie had dreams of being healthy, it seemed like she was in a rather hopeless situation. New knees would allow her to exercise more to lose the weight, but the docs wanted her to lose the weight before getting the new knees.

Cathie's husband also "acted older" than he was, having been diagnosed with chronic fatigue syndrome. When I arrived at their home, it didn't take me long to figure out why Cathie was showing up in life the way she was. Her home gave the impression that people around 85 or 90 years old lived there! She had an overabundance of "inherited" furnishings and objects from her long-dead ancestors arranged in such a way that the home felt old, tired, and slooooow. If you moved too fast, you might knock an antique-filled shadowbox off the wall.

As I proceeded through the house, I noticed a little picture of a couple of hippies (daisies and all) looking very happy. I asked "Who's this?" She said, "That's us on our wedding day!" So I said, "Where did the hippies go?"

Well, that was all it took to awaken Cathie to her situation of having built an environment for people MUCH older than she was and MUCH slower than she wanted to be. She started painting the antiques bright "hippie color combinations" and de-cluttering the things that did not align with her dream of being fit and healthy—like the Civil War reenactment "spinner" costume and props I found under the bed.

She joined a gym, hired a trainer, and told him that kayaking was going to be her thing (as it took arms, not legs, and because she could continue doing that while she got her knees replaced). She started working out her arms and kayaking. Her trainer became her kayaking partner, and long story short, she lost the weight, won kayaking competitions, and has new knees and a whole new healthy life.

When I returned to her home several years later (she's in her 60's now), I couldn't believe what I saw. Besides all the bright, fresh, and happy-feeling colors and contemporary furnishings, she had all sorts of kayaks, paddles, clothing racks full of drying wet suits, protein goo-packs, and caps from all the races she had entered. Her stuff had completely changed! She didn't have one cap before, nor would she have considered wearing one!

I asked her, "If I had told you in the beginning, back in that antique-stuffed house, that what you needed around there were some kayaks, wet suits, and goo packs, what would you have said?" She replied, "I would have said, 'you are CRAZY!'" But as you can see, I wouldn't have been—as that was the very stuff that helped her create the reality of being a healthy, fit kayaking competitor. I'm not saying to clutter it up or anything, but at the very least, it's worthwhile to honor your Dream Life. Cathie said that the change happened slowly over time, but it *did* happen because of her committed vision (that's good old Providence working for ya!) and her willingness (high-ranking emotional vibe!) to continue moving forward toward her dream. So, please don't hold yourself back here. Dream it and then start to build it—even if it seems impossible. You don't need to know how it all ends right now.

Chapter 4: Balance Your Body

It's hard to feel the earlier list of high-vibrating feelings when your physical body is out of whack. Thus, in this chapter, I present my favorite body balancers. For some people, making a physical body shift will be an easy task, and for others, it might be more of a grandiose adventure. If you are of the latter camp, I propose a kinder, gentler approach of easing into the process slowly, as this will make your endeavors, shall I say, more palatable.

What IS your body, anyway? The physical matter, energy, and genetic makeup you were given at birth PLUS what you ate, drank, inhaled, ingested, injected, absorbed, sniffed, snorted, believed, perceived, and were exposed to MINUS everything you have eliminated EQUALS your current physical body.

The issues of the body center around managing intake and output—simple as that. But in order to create a healthy body, you must be "in-the-know" about certain aspects of what affects what. The following shifting techniques and information present gentle ways of being mindful and honoring the body, so it can serve you in return. Shifting the course of your physical structure to run more optimally will, among other things, help you identify with more positive outcomes in life, draw your optimal healthy future toward you, and support your mind and spirit while you apply other techniques in this book.

The balancing of your physical body is really helpful to maximize your journey's efforts, as it's the one "house" from which you can't move—

in this lifetime at least! If this idea seems depressing or overwhelming (or otherwise negative), go back to Chapter 2 to identify and deal with that reaction. It is of no importance, no significance, nor truth. You are a person of unlimited potential, so when you have reactions that undermine that potential, you know you are in the counsel of lowly, counterproductive, and unnecessary thought forms. Rid yourself of them, and allow the breeze of possibility to blow through what was once a tightly knit web of subversive thoughts.

For practicality and priority purposes, take a moment to figure out and list the *minimum basic needs* that support your body. Air, water, sleep, and nutritious food should all be on the list, right? Life gets quickly unbalanced without enough of these, even though they usually aren't even on the radar until something or someone takes them away.

Perhaps there are additional must-haves that keep you balanced. How much exercise, personal hygiene time, meditation, yoga, sex, alone time, laughter, time in nature, sports, puttering around time, affection, quality company, travel and adventure, volunteer time, or appreciation do you need to feel healthy and balanced? Are there other must-haves on your personal list?

Go ahead and create that list now. State each item, how much of it you require, and how often you need it. Remember, this is the minimum requirement, without which you would be off balance or unwell—not the ultimate or "dream amount."[1] Follow the example below to create your list:

What I Need	How Much	For How Long
Sleep	6.5 hours	per night
Water	32 ounces	per day
Eating healthy meals	3 times	per day
Laughing out loud	1 time	per day
Quality company	4 hours	per week
Hobby/creativity time	2 hours	per week
Travel/adventure	1 big trip and 5 local	per year
Alone time	3.5 hours	per week
Sex & physical intimacy	4 times	per month
Seeing beauty/time in nature	1 time	per week

Now, if you can imagine having all of your physical needs met, wouldn't you be better equipped to create and live out your ultimate Dream Life? Work the "If You Build It" Enhancer, and make sure you have the physical environment necessary to support the basic needs you have listed here. You will find yourself complaining less and loving your life more.

I cannot tell you how important it is to consider all four aspects of your life simultaneously. Do not allow any aspect—mind, body, spirit, or living and work environments—to go complacently unnoticed, as that area will eventually become your Achilles' heel. Honoring all aspects of life will lead you to the great wonders of your optimal potential.

Some words of advice before diving into this material: knowledge is power. Relax. Keep your thoughts and emotions at a high level. This is not about getting overwhelmed and locked up over every little thing that could possibly be done to potentially improve your health. It is about knowing your weak links and generating the simplest changes that have the best potential to shift you. It is also about considering options and becoming more mindful of what you allow in your home, so you have to generate fewer additional shifts in the future.

OK, with chill-pill popped . . . you can continue. Make sure your notebook is handy for your health-generating list of Body Balancers.

The Air Quality Balancers

This Balancer addresses the "exposed to" and "inhaled" part of the body makeup and also includes environmental changes. But before we begin, take a moment to picture the Dream Life you wrote down. Now, fill the air of that picture with sooty black pollution from lead chips, pesticides, and off-gassing plastics. Does that life seem optimal now?

I know you probably weren't expecting a conversation on air quality, but healthy bodies and lives don't last long at all without good air. Most people don't think about the subject until their good air is taken away, but as your future picture just showed you, healthy air is a must for living optimally. And yes, we're going beyond the "please don't smoke" conversation. That should be a given.

Did you know that the Environmental Protection Agency ranks poor indoor air quality among the top five environmental risks to public health? They cite that air pollution **in the home** is often 2 to 5, and occasionally up to 100 times higher than outdoor levels.[2] To be clear, we're not talking about shutting down the coal plant on the other side of town first. We're talking about dealing with what is closest to you and working your way outward.

If you are remodeling or building, you may consider choosing an LEED-certified architect and/or builder to ensure that this kind of thought goes into the building material choices for your new place. If you are in an existing structure and you or someone living with you has a lung problem or other chronic health issue, I'd recommend having the air in your home professionally tested to see if there is some invisible something working against you. Alternatively, you can buy home tests and do a lot of the testing yourself. But even if you are healthy, I'd recommend being mindful in the ways described below, as these suggestions can potentially save you from a respiratory problem or other chronic health issue in the future.

1. Change and Upgrade Filters

I have to throw this one in, because as easy, uncomplicated, inexpensive, and lung-helpful as it is, many people do not replace their heating and air conditioning filters as recommended—if at all! The industry term for the standard heater filter that comes with typical systems is a "boulder catcher," which does not filter enough for optimal health. So, consider this no-brainer to increase indoor air quality: upgrade your heating filter and change it as recommended. Use a minimum "merv 11" filter or better. Use HEPA-filtered air purifiers if you currently have lung issues (keeping a six- to eight-foot distance from their electromagnetic fields, of course).

2. Mitigate or Minimize Off-Gassing of Volatile Organic Compounds (VOC's)

There are many chemicals that get emitted into your home's air on a regular basis. This emissions process is called "off-gassing." Some common invisible airborne chemicals emitted include acetone, benzene, formaldehyde, phthalates, and polyvinyl chloride (also known as PVC). These emissions come from everyday items in the home, including synthetic carpet and materials, window blinds, dishes, furniture, binder covers, solvents, household cleaning fluids, pesticides, office equipment, paint remover, flame retardant coatings on fabrics, foam cushions and prefab items found in mobile homes, particleboard and chipboard, wallpaper, auto interiors, dyes, laundry pre-spot treatments, wrinkle treatments, baby bottles, vinyl shower curtains and table cloths, preservatives, plastics, construction building materials, and even some perfumes. (If you've ever smelled that "new car smell" or "new doll smell," you've experienced off-gassing.) And because homes are built so air-tight these days, these VOC's don't have much of a chance to escape or become diluted.

Why do you care? Because health issues like asthma, concentration and memory problems, cancer, birth defects, brain damage, multiple chemical sensitivity, organ damage and failure, depression, fatigue, watering eyes, stinging nose, central nervous system problems, and more are all linked to VOC exposure.[3]

My advice here is to be cautious of what new products you bring into your home. If I have to go on record, I'd say that synthetic carpeting is the biggest polluter by volume, and a vinyl shower curtain is the nastiest smaller item—just to start naming names. Would you have guessed it? I'm naming names to get you to think about COMMON stuff that we innocently add to our environments without so much as one investigatory thought. What about caulking, facial tissues, or those stinky felt-tipped markers? What exactly makes that smell in fabric softeners, dryer sheets, and air "fresheners?" What about disposable diapers on your baby? If something is releasing a smell and it is going into your nose, you have to think about the fallout from that exposure.

The manufacturing process of PVC is probably *the* most toxic manufacturing process of all, creating the deadly chemical called *dioxin*. So, if you want to vote with your wallet, vote against buying PVC, plastic, and vinyl products and you'll do yourself and the planet a favor.

Choose natural materials or untreated materials if you can. If you're re-insulating, demand formaldehyde-free insulation. Ask questions and dig for answers. Read labels. Research the material safety data sheet (MSDS) available online for a specific product. You might be shocked at what you find. Just because it is made and sold does not necessarily mean it is safe for you. Also, ventilate your home every once in a while by opening all the windows and changing the air the good ol' fashioned way. If you do bring a new item into the home—especially if it smells—I'd step up your ventilation game.

If you want to bring in some natural (and pretty!) "chemical-treatment plants," try these plants for starters. There are others as well, if you do some research.

- **Boston Fern** (*Nephrolepsis exaltata bostoniensis*)—removes formaldehyde and xylene well. Place one or two in each room that has new furniture or carpeting in it.
- **English Ivy** (*Hedera helix*)—removes benzene, formaldehyde, and xylene. This plant is great for freshly painted rooms and rooms that house plastic equipment, such as printers and computers.
- **Areca Palm** (*Chrysalidocarpus lutescens*)—removes xylene, toluene, and formaldehyde. This plant is good for rooms with new furniture.
- **Spider plant** (*Chlorophytum cosmosum*) —removes carbon monoxide, xylene, and formaldehyde. This plant is great near gas stoves and in rooms with fireplaces or anywhere that carbon monoxide may accumulate.
- **Janet Craig / Striped Dracena** (*Dracaena deremensis*)—removes formaldehyde and xylene, which is good for newly furnished and newly carpeted areas.
- **Peace Lily** (*Spathiphyllum cochlearispathum*)—removes benzene and formaldehyde. Place in rooms that contain household cleaners, pesticides, lighter fluids, hydraulic fluids, solvents . . . oh, there are so many! If you aren't "going green" on every product you bring into your home (which I recommend), you've probably got benzene somewhere![4]

3. Check and Balance Humidity Levels

The US Environmental Protection Agency suggests that a healthy home's humidity level is between 30 and 50 percent.[5] A simple test using a "hygrometer" (purchased online, or from electronic, high-tech, or hardware stores) can show you what humidity level you've got at any given moment. Anything consistently over, say, 53 percent may give you health problems as that sets up the right conditions for mold to grow to a toxic level in the home. And if that isn't bad enough, VOC's out-gas at a higher rate and biological contaminants thrive and proliferate at higher humidity levels.

The top common sources of high humidity are poorly ventilated bathrooms, laundry rooms, kitchens, and water vapor emissions from a floor slab. If you have water running down inside your windows, you've got too much humidity. If it smells musty in your home (ask a friend) or if you see mildew, you've got too much humidity. Check under the refrigerator, behind sinks, in the basement, around dryer vents, and on ceilings for signs of excess moisture.

Bathrooms usually collect humidity because people only run the fan while they are in the bathroom—which is usually too little. One way to handle that is to install a 100 CFM fan and put it on a timer switch. Then, each time someone takes a shower or a hot bath, they can turn on the dial for one hour and not have to worry about turning it off after they leave the room. And obviously, if you have a window, use it—but the window alone is not always sufficient.

Kitchens and laundry rooms can add water vapors in the home through cooking, dishwashing, and clothes laundering. Use outdoor-vented exhaust fans in the kitchen and laundry room. Always vent clothes dryers to the outdoors. Open windows and ventilate when and where you can.

If you can't figure out the source of your high humidity, my guess would be that you have high water vapor emissions from a floor slab. Most people only find this out after their wooden floors buckle up, or their tile keeps popping off the slab. But some homes hide their vapor emission symptoms well. There is a test for this type of problem and yes, there are slab sealers for it. So, it is fixable. This may be a situation where there is a tradeoff involved: adding a synthetic chemical sealer to the home to fix the air quality in the home—you make the call. (The good news here is that you usually place some type of flooring over the slab, so direct contact with the sealer doesn't happen.)

If you notice a correlation between the time of year when you close all the windows and turn on the heat or air conditioner and the time of year when you have increased doctor's visits, I'd guess it's your house making you sick, not "the weather." Make your own house call.

4. Clean Up Your Cleaning and Pest-Control Products

This one's fairly simple. If there is a health hazard warning on the label, it's a health hazard. Hmmmm, what's going on in your house is going on in your life, you say . . . .

I received an e-mail from a gal reporting in on her newfound connection between her stuff and her life, from a feng shui perspective. She noticed that she had all of her toxic cleaning and pest control supplies under her kitchen cabinet in the relationship *gua* of her house (the back, right-hand part from where you enter through the front door). She then went on to make the connection about the toxic men she kept attracting who "bugged her," to say the least. After swift removal of the supplies, a swift change in the quality of men happened, too.

I applaud this gal for making that connection! She was definitely wearing her feng shui glasses. Not only would I expect her to see improvement in her relationships, but I'd look for a healthier kitchen and healthier food energy because of the "cleaner environment" around her food, cooking equipment, and water.

Start experimenting with more environmentally and health-friendly products, and start switching to the brands you like the best. And if you have some unexplained illness, get this higher up on the to-do list.

5. Avoid Combustion Gasses

I'm talking about deadly carbon monoxide here, so pay attention! The most common sources for these gasses indoors are gas stoves, hot water heaters, furnaces, fireplaces, and of course, vehicles in the garage. Make sure you have working combustion gas/carbon monoxide detectors in the home. Turn on the overhead vent the entire time you are cooking, and preferably open a window for added measure if the weather allows. Chronic headaches, blurred vision, and drowsiness may occur if you are exposed to combustion gasses. If you can't figure out why you've got these symptoms, call a plumber to check your appliances. Call the gas company if you smell gas.

Here are some additional unhealthy gasses of note. Methane gas comes from compost piles, farm animals, leaky sewer lines, defective household sink and bath drains, and termites. (What? Yep! They have the capacity to emit combustible materials into YOUR living space!) Tobacco smoke also emits toxic gasses. Proximity to power plants may be an issue as well.

6. Avoid Lead Exposure

Lead negatively affects the brain, kidneys, liver, and bones and is especially hazardous to children and pregnant women. Before 1978, house paint often included lead, so inhalation of lead particles found in the dust of older homes or in debris from the demolition of these homes is common. (Children can chew on trim paint and other painted surfaces as well as simply inhaling lead particles via the dust created by window and door-jamb friction.) Also, peeling paint containing lead may be vacuumed up and then re-circulated into the air.[6]

Lead invades our drinking water in the solder that the plumber uses to join the pipes and faucets. Run water for about 20 seconds before placing the glass under the faucet—especially first thing in the morning—to drain off any water that might have possibly been touching solder or Teflon tape (which has PVC in it).

There are many inexpensive lead detection and testing kits that you can purchase in home improvement stores to find out if your safety is in jeopardy.

Reverse osmosis water filtration at the point of use (such as the kitchen sink) can help to prevent water contamination by lead as well as other sources.

7. Avoid Asbestos

Basically, if your home was built prior to 1978, you may have some asbestos in a building material somewhere: ceiling tiles, insulation, etc. Asbestos was banned from use in many building materials in the 1970s, but in some materials such as floor tile, its use wasn't banned until 1989. If you have asbestos in your home, it must be removed by professionals. It causes irreversible lung damage, including lung cancer.

8. Avoid Radon

Radon is a colorless, odorless, invisible radioactive soil gas that is a byproduct of the decay of uranium. It is a relatively harmless gas when it is in outdoor air. Unfortunately, with today's tightly sealed houses, radon can get trapped indoors. It is the second largest cause of lung cancer after smoking—so it's worth checking out!

Radon gets into homes through cracks in flooring, crawl spaces, or anywhere the building touches the earth. It can be reduced by increasing ventilation, sealing the areas where the house contacts soil, or installing a sub-slab suction system that pulls the soil gasses out of the living space. This system must be installed by professionals, as they can test to ensure optimal air quality. Even though these testing and mitigation efforts are expensive, they are probably a fraction of the costs of lung cancer treatment—so please do your homework to see if radon remediation is something you need to do.

9. Avoid Dust and Particulate Matter

We're down to dust in the air as a possible health risk factor.

Poor quality vacuum cleaners can put more dust in the air than they take off of the floors. Couple that with wall-to-wall carpet, and you've got a bad combination. Fireplace drafting can also be increasing particulate matter in the air, as can a high pollen count outside that ends up "walking" in the door.

Here's a simple answer to dust and particulate matter: clean! Do you know how many homes I go into where there is visible dust sitting on top of curtains and furnishings in the house? Well, you can guess that not only are they stuck in life as far as opportunities go, but they also usually have some sort of (at least minor) lung issue as a complaint. As I stated in the last chapter, cleaning IS feng shui-ing your home. Maybe if you think of it like that, you will be more proactive for your health, wealth, and happiness.

How's that chill pill doing? Remember, knowledge is power.

The Water Quality Balancer

How much of your body is water? A lot! And since the World Health Organization estimates that the cost of disease in the world related to contaminated water is over $260 billion per year, I cannot ignore water quality as a discussion topic, even though most of you reading this are in your comfortable homes with running water on tap at the flip of a handle.[7] (Everything is ONE energy, remember?) I'm sure most readers here haven't given water quality much thought, but nonetheless, it must be considered if you are to be creating optimal healthy living spaces and bodies. In the US, the Safe Drinking Water Act lists inorganic contaminants and their maximum allowable levels, if you want to do some light reading on that subject.

If you are aware of what you are really drinking (inorganic contaminants like cadmium, fluoride, thallium, mercury, beryllium, arsenic, antimony, and selenium, along with solvents, pesticides, herbicides, PCB's, oh and let's not forget radioactive decay and chlorine), you might be able to connect the dots between your water and the issues these materials cause in our bodies: cancer, kidney, lung, central nervous system, endocrine, and heart issues, to name a few. A specific contaminant may or may not be the one thing creating your health issue, but it may be at least one of the contributing components, or it may be what's making your condition chronic. There are MANY possible contaminants, but I wanted to chat about a couple of them to enlighten you on how this stuff gets inside your body.

Since plastics are everywhere these days—let's stop drinking hot drinks from polystyrene cups and reduce our dependence on drinks from plastic bottles, shall we?—it may be no surprise that the phthalates and nonylphenol that make up plastics are in the water, too. In many places, these contaminants are in the ground water supply without a plastic bottle in sight! Although natural filtering through soil used to be one of our best water filtration methods, over-contamination has lessened the soil's ability to effectively do its job. But soil filtration aside, you might be giving yourself a "direct injection" of chemicals by drinking straight from the cup or plastic bottle.

Here are a few additional considerations:

1. If you own a well, get some testing done to learn what types of contaminants exist and at what levels, and mitigate accordingly. Also, test at your tap to make sure that copper and lead levels from the plumbing are not adding more contaminants in the harmful range.
2. If you have city water, look up the latest water quality report in your water district and see if there are any known contaminants. If you look up health issues caused by these contaminants, it may help you connect the dots between your lack of health and your water.
3. There are many ways to clean up your water, depending on what you find in it. (There are tests if you want to go that far.) Consider installing tap filters, such as charcoal filters, and whole house water systems, such as reverse osmosis filters, to remove as many contaminants as possible. That sneaky chlorine is even getting into your body through your skin in the shower, so just using tap filters is not catching it all.

Congratulations on hanging in there with me for that "Debbie Downer" information. It's now time for the food!

The Dining Space Balancer

If you're going to eat well, maximize your shift by eating in a well-feng shuied space. Enhancing your eating environment can literally improve your health energy. And who doesn't want good health energy? All too often, I have seen situations where people eat in the car and at their desk because they simply have not created a better space to slow down and eat. Imagine these two scenes and tell me who is living life to the fullest: (1) a person eating a taco from the bag while driving and being honked at from behind; or (2) a person sitting at a tablecloth-covered table with a lovely view and nice music playing in the background? What judgments do you make about these people just from reading those descriptions? Notice the internal conversations and "Modernize" whatever doesn't work for you.

If you eat most often in the car or at your desk, do not pass go and do not collect the bag from the drive-through window. If you believe you don't have the time to eat well, employ your Helpful People Box with a note of thanks about the time you now have to honor your body by purchasing and preparing healthy foods. Volunteer your time in order to "prime the pump" and get the "give to receive" energies working for you in the time department (there's more up ahead on this one!), or Energy Transfer Modernize the story in your head about how it isn't possible given your schedule, or other people or things are more important than your health.

Here are the basic components of a decent dining space: a chair, a flat eating surface to place the food on so you are not holding it, and light. Not so hard, right? Now, if you want to "up" the quality of the experience, make sure you have: a comfortable chair; a solid (not glass) table in proportion to the chair that works well—not too high, not too low, etc.; natural light in addition to overhead light; and no clutter or distractions (a.k.a. a TV!) within eye-shot. If you have a glass table, place a table cloth over it, or use placemats at a minimum.

Now, if you want to really feel good while eating, include everything above plus: beautiful dishes and flatware, fresh flowers, a candle, a cloth napkin, fresh air flow, and possibly beautiful art or another visually pleasing (not animated like a TV) view. Depending on your taste, soft music in the background might be a good addition.

Some other things to think about include having a chair at the table for every member of the household, whether you ever eat all together or not (this could be a situation where you are not because the chairs are not allowing the possibility of it), and possibly keeping living objects like plants or fresh fruit in your dining location to keep fresh, vital life force energy nearby.

One final comment: the dining room space is a relationship-building space no matter where it is in the house. So, if you don't see the point in improving the space because you eat alone, you might want to make it a point to bolster this space even more to attract company with which to dine.

The Food Quality Balancer

Before you find out what kinds of foods work best for you in the upcoming section, let's discuss what *qualities* of foods work best for you. The following is by no means an all-inclusive list, but if you have never really made the connection between foods and health, this list from my friend and healing nutrition teacher Melanie Ferreira is a good one to use to start the process of healthier eating.[8]

1. The more natural, fresh, whole, and unprocessed, the better. Buy locally grown foods as well as seasonal foods, as they will be your best bet for nutrients. Do your best to avoid canned, sprayed, waxed, bioengineered, or irradiated fruits, vegetables, spices, and herbs.
2. Choose organic, grass-fed versus grain-fed lamb and beef. Organic livestock are raised on organic pastures and are not

administered hormones or antibiotics. These meats have more omega-3 fatty acids and actually contain skin-helpful conjugated lineolic acid.

3. Choose wild-caught fish instead of farmed fish, as the farmed varieties include soy and corn feed and often dye to brighten the skin of the fish. Fish farming is also hard on the environment. Wild-caught fish have a higher omega-3 fatty acid profile as well. If heavy metal contaminants are a concern, avoid fish known to be high in mercury, such as tuna and swordfish.
4. Choose free-range, organic, and pasture-fed chicken and eggs.
5. Prepare stocks from animal bones to capture the valuable nutrition released into the stocks from the bones. Bone broth is an excellent immune system booster.
6. Be sure to soak all beans, nuts, and grains before consuming or preparing them to neutralize phytic acid and enzyme inhibitors. Phytic acid interferes with the body's absorption of iron, magnesium, calcium, and zinc. It is found in unsoaked grains and nuts and all non-fermented soy products, including soy milk and tofu.
7. Avoid soy protein isolate (read labels!). Many chemicals are used in the manufacturing process, which also involves high heat, rendering the protein nutritionally useless and at the same time increasing its levels of nitrates and carcinogens.
8. It is best to buy organic wheat products, as non-organic wheat is heavily sprayed with pesticides. Purchase your grain flour as fresh as possible—possibly even grinding your own.
9. Use sea salt instead of regular table salt, as it includes many health-supporting minerals.
10. Cook with organic extra virgin coconut oil for many reasons, including heart health. Coconut oil is high in lauric acid,

which boosts the immune system and helps fight against infections.

11. Avoid hydrogenated and partially hydrogenated oils. Among other things, these oils raise LDL and lower HDL cholesterols. They are often catalyzed with contaminating metals in a process that thickens them and prevents them from spoiling. The end result is, essentially, one step away from plastic.
12. Use only natural sweeteners like organic grade B maple syrup, raw honey, stevia, agave, and brown rice syrup.
13. Consume or prepare foods with sea vegetables in your diet for added minerals. Sea vegetables include the sheets of *nori* that you use to wrap sushi, as well as others in various shapes and textures, including *kombu*, *arame*, and *hijiki*. (I drop a piece of kombu in the pot just about every time I boil liquids.)
14. Consume unpasteurized beer and wine if you happen to drink.
15. Consume lacto-fermented beverages and foods daily to add healthy bacteria to your diet and aid digestion. These foods include kefir and sauerkraut. (Debbie Downer alert: if it is pasteurized, you're not eating the right stuff! Debbie Upper alert: if you eat the real stuff, it helps kill sugar cravings!)
16. Avoid synthetic vitamins and foods containing them.
17. Avoid food additives (like MSG), hydrolyzed vegetable protein, and artificial sweeteners (like aspartame), as they are neurotoxins.
18. Avoid aluminum-containing foods like baking powder, salt, and antacids. (Avoid using aluminum cookware and aluminum-containing deodorants too!) Aluminum has been linked to multiple health issues, including Alzheimer's disease and breast cancer.[9]

If you are overwhelmed by the above list, remember, small changes over a long period of time will get you to your goal. But the more pain you have and the unhealthier you feel, the faster I would incorporate these quality Balancers into your life.

The Yin and Yang Food Balancer

Now that we've covered food quality, we're going to move more deeply into the food conversation. Are you ready to tweak your diet to shift your life?

Mindset check! Did anything negative just go through your head? Is anything stopping you from totally getting on board with this? Are you starting to feel any resistance to the ideas in this chapter? If a negative or unresourceful "mental tape" just played, you've got Mind Modernizing work to do.

You say you can't control your cravings? Challenge that thought. Up your emotional vibration by doing the Climb the Ladder of Emotions Modernizer. You don't think you are capable of sticking to a healthy lifestyle? Do an Energy Transfer Modernizer on that one. Everything that could derail you starts in the mind, so challenge it—and get past what once appeared to be a permanent road block. Turns out, it was just an erroneously placed sign along the road to success.

Yin and Yang Qualities

Like everything else on the planet, you can place each food item somewhere along the line that describes it as more yin or more yang. Here's a recap of yin and yang descriptions again to get the conversation rolling.

Yin qualities are usually: darker, colder, wetter, rougher, softer, cushier, quieter, more contracted, smaller, more inward, more receptive, more feminine, floral, rounder, or more curved.

Yang qualities are typically: lighter, hotter, dryer, smoother, harder, sharper, louder, more expansive, larger, more outward-moving and dispersing, more active, more masculine, striped or plaid, and straighter or more angular.

Now, you can see from these definition lists that some descriptions can easily pertain to food, like wetter or harder or darker, right? Also, remember that everything usually has both yin and yang qualities at some level. For example, how would you describe a coconut? It is very wet inside and round, which is yin, but it also has a very hard shell, which is yang. The following illustration shows food categories from a Traditional Chinese Medicine (TCM) yin and yang standpoint:[10]

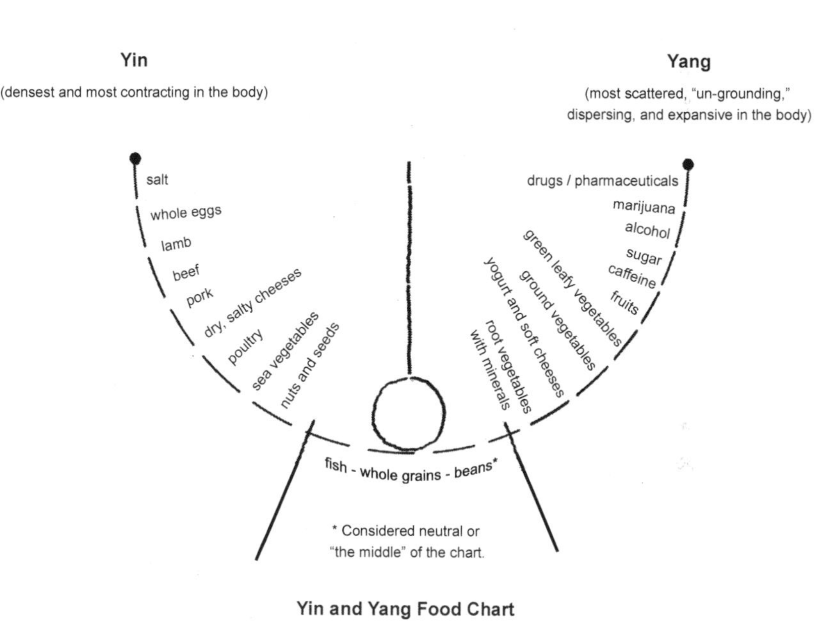

Yin and Yang Food Chart
Figure 20

Considering this illustration, do you consistently consume more yin or yang foods? Or do you perhaps eat from both ends, but rarely from the center? You might want to do some food journaling if you are unsure. Get familiar with the types (from a yin and yang standpoint) and quantities (by percentage) of the foods you eat by listing them in your notebook, so when you want to make some adjustments and substitutions to your diet, you'll quickly know which way to go.

Food Cravings

Have you ever eaten a heavy meal like a steak, and then craved a sweet dessert like, say, chocolate afterwards? How about a burger and fries that have to be followed up with a hot fudge sundae? What's going on here is that the body is naturally craving a food item from the other end of the yin and yang chart to neutralize or counterbalance what you just ate. This is also the reason why many people love snacks and desserts that are both sweet and salty.

To reduce or eliminate your cravings, eat a more neutral diet. That means the majority of your food intake should come from "the middle" of the yin and yang chart. The items that are considered in the middle or the most neutral are beans, whole grains, and fish.

If you just got a little sad after hearing that information, remember that small changes and substitutions over time will more surely and smoothly lead to a healthier lifestyle. For example, the average person eats three meals a day, right? So start with breakfast changes. If you start the day "neutral," eating whole grains or other foods from the center of the chart, chances are you'll have more success at staying neutral throughout the day. But even if you don't, you've changed 33.3% of your intake and eaten at least one neutral meal. That's progress!

By the way, when I say whole grains, I'm thinking of non-processed, natural, or "bulk bin"-type grains. Chances are that if it has a brand name other than the mill it came from, it's somehow processed. There are lots of choices out there these days—it's not as hard as you might think to find these good grains.

As long as we're talking grains, use the following tips to choose the most helpful grains for you:[11]

- If you know that you have liver or gallbladder issues, poor

eyesight, or a tendency toward anger or irritability, you might consider eating barley, oats, and wheat.
- For those of you who have heart or small intestine issues, have a poor sense of smell perhaps, or are overrun with feelings of sadness, you might consider a ground milled corn product.
- For those of you with stomach and spleen issues, taste problems, or an abundance of blame, guilt, or worry, choose millet.
- If you have lung weaknesses of any kind or issues with your large intestine, or if you have a consistently depressed outlook, the grains rice, quinoa, and amaranth would be good choices.
- If you suffer from kidney, bladder, or hearing issues, or have a great deal of fear, choose buckwheat. You should also respond well to beans.

Now that you've got your grain or grains chosen, follow these preparation tips:

1. SOAKING: Before you go to bed at night, take about a quarter to a half of a cup of your grains, put them in a pan, and add good filtered water—just enough to cover the grains so they can soak. Usually, if there are no pest problems in your house, you can just keep the pan right on the stove until it's time to cook the grains in the morning. Unlike beans, which you soak prior to cooking as well, you don't change or throw out the water when soaking grains because you'd lose the minerals that escaped the grains. But you do want to soak them, because in soaking grains, you are allowing the phytic acid to be released. Phytic acid blocks mineral absorption, and it will evaporate as the grains cook. (After soaking beans, though, definitely do toss out the bean water!)

2. COOKING: Before cooking, add a pinch of good sea salt, turn on the stove, and cook your grains and water.
3. FLAVORING: Once cooked, you can add things like dried fruits, natural sweeteners, and a little cream (if you tolerate dairy) to flavor your grains. However, I would not recommend brown sugar, white sugar, or anything from the far ends of the yin and yang chart other than the pinch of salt. As you get used to this meal, you will see that your need for sweetening lessens.

The traditional word for this type of grain breakfast is "congee" or "jook," so feel free to find recipes online that might have combinations that sound good to you, or that you know will be helpful considering your body type, which we'll discuss next. Some recipes include meats, for those of you who may need a little more protein in your diet to keep you going until lunch.

Like I said, if you change this "one-third of your daily meals" to neutral foods, you'll start to see your cravings lessen and even disappear. Then, once you get breakfast stabilized, you can start working on your other meals and snacks.

Know Your Body Type

If you know your specific "constitution," you'll be able to get more specific with balancing your meals using the yin and yang food chart. The following are the four most common body types described with the traditional yin and yang names.

The first body type is called **Excess Yang**. People with an excess yang constitution look overheated, they may have a ruddy appearance, their skin is usually coarse, and they have a muscular framework. Some might describe them as "beefy." They have a tendency to have:

- excess weight;
- thick, bushy, wiry hair;
- possibly a strong body odor;

- a full or barrel-shaped chest;
- an arrogant attitude; and
- a slow metabolism.

If you were to ask them if they had many childhood illnesses, they would say no. Think construction worker here—a physically strong, steak-and-potato type. Another way to describe this body type is a "heart attack on a plate." They love rich foods, and are usually the ones to have heart attacks at young ages—like 45 or younger.

Foods that could support the Excess Yang body type include: quick stir-fries, whole grains, seafood, raw foods, and salads. If any alcohol is involved at all, it should be cooked with the food. This is perhaps the only body type that can tolerate fasting (a couple of days here and there during the spring or summer months). Foods that Excess Yang body types should usually avoid are: coffee, liquor, junk food (carbs and sweets), baked goods, flour, hard cheeses, meats—especially fire-grilled meats—peppers, and spices. And, believe it or not because it seems counter-intuitive given our list, they should limit salt intake.

The next body type is called **Excess Yin**. People with this constitution have a heavier, thick structure but not coarse skin. Their skin is soft, delicate, and usually pale. Unlike the Excess Yang body type, Excess Yin bodies carry excess weight but are "spongy" rather than having the Excess Yang's underlying muscle tone. They usually sweat, have edema or excess water, and are slower and not as "athletic" and strong as Excess Yang types.

Excess Yin bodies would be helped by cooked fruits, stir-fries, cooked greens, brown rice, adzuki beans, watercress and salads, and herbs and spices like ginger, garlic, rosemary, cinnamon, and basil.

This body type should avoid still starches (a.k.a. "couch potatoes"), dairy, white foods, processed foods, raw or frozen foods, cool foods and drinks, excess liquids, hard cheeses, cold smoothies, and once again, seemingly counter-intuitive—beef and lamb.

This body type can also use more exercise to move and transform the "still" energies sitting upon it, as lack of movement is a big culprit in this imbalance.

The third body type is called **Yin Deficient.** This body type has a fast metabolism and is usually thin—at least thinner than the Excess Yin type. They often have dryness, insomnia, poor concentration, and restlessness or the appearance of not being "anchored." Their energy level is good, but their substance is weak. They usually have a lightheaded feeling or are crabby when they haven't eaten. They might have hot hands and cheeks. If I were to sum up this body type, I would say that they are the type that "burns the candle at both ends."

This body type should incorporate more grains, root vegetables, potatoes, oils, heavier foods, coconut oil and coconut milk, thicker soups and casseroles, clams, mussels, deep-sea fish, sauces, and eggs. They can also tolerate good dairy products.

They should avoid caffeine, sugar, spicy foods, nicotine, and alcohol.

The fourth body type is called **Moderate Yang.** This body type is athletic with good muscle tone and well-nourished skin—like a healthy teenager body. My dietary recommendations are: avoid an excess of anything. If you are any of the other three body types, aim to be this one.

Yin and Yang Moods

Adding another layer onto the yin and yang chart are specific emotions and attitudes. See if you can figure out a personal connection to these and make additional food choice adjustments to up your emotional vibe. There is a lot to consider, and sometimes things seem contradictory. If that is the case with you, I'd suggest simply making one change at a time to see if it seems right for you. Change something for 27 days and then look back and notice the shift.

Yin moods: depressed, sad, down, quiet, lonely, receptive, introverted, passive, undisciplined, artistically and spiritually inclined, still, and philosophic.

Yang moods: boisterous, loud, materialistic, socially inclined, aggressive, and forceful.

Coupled with the body types, these attitudes may hold further clues as to where imbalances are in your diet.

Knowing the yin and yang food chart, body types, and your current diet, can you make helpful connections and devise changes and substitutions to shift your body toward balance?

When I do nutritional counseling with my clients, I usually look to make minor substitutions first and then work in any major changes that need to happen. I balance their breakfast and then work on the other meals and snacks. This approach works better when making a long-term lifestyle change than attempting a big, crash diet that you fall off of quickly. You might also want to reconsider the feng shui of your home and workplace yin and yang shifts to further support your specific yin and yang body type needs.

The Five-Element Food and Mood Balancer

Describing the five elements is really a discussion about energy and the circle of life. Once you understand it, you can apply the concept to anything—your room, your home, your property, and so on. But for now, let's use it to help you understand food energy, so you'll have the strength and stamina for that robust, intimate love life, better-paying job, vibrant health, or whatever else you are inviting in and preparing to have in your life very soon. (Mindset check! Did any unresourceful thoughts just go through your mind after reading that last sentence? If so, unwind and remove them using the Mind Modernizer of your choice. You should be getting used to these techniques by now!)

One Energy Equals Five Elements

Remember the "Everything is Energy" premise? Every single thing that you see is one thing—energy. And energy has many different expressions. In order to effectively communicate these expressions in a useful way, we can mentally divide this thing called energy into five parts. These parts are the five stages of energy as it transforms in time. Some people simply call the five elements "five energies going," which more clearly defines the "ever-going" personality of life energy. Around and around and around it goes. That's just the way it works. Nothing is static. There's no getting around it. Cells divide and die off. Apple peels and coffee grounds turn into fertilizer when composted, and so on. Your body was slightly different yesterday than it is today.

Just as someone millennia ago figured out the positive- and negative-resulting feng shui arrangements and patterns and how they affect us, someone figured out that our biological bodies function best in the presence of particular vibrating energy patterns positioned in specific locations. The five-element concept is just another universal pattern—like the organization of the colors in a rainbow, for example. Once you know the five elements, you'll be able to easily understand how to accommodate them in your diet as well as how to position them in your environment.

There are five specific vibratory patterns. Their movements are:

- Downward
- Expanding
- Upward
- Horizontal
- Contracting

These five movements were given the following names and descriptions to make conversing about them easier.

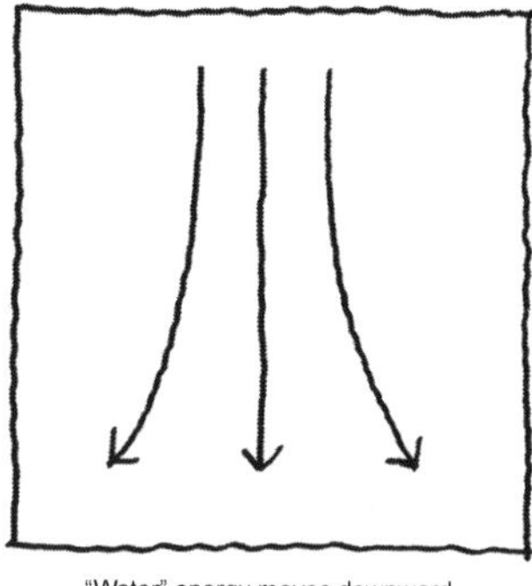

"Water" energy moves downward

Figure 21

The first movement consists of *downward* moving molecules. It is referred to as "water," because it is reminiscent of the rain falling from the sky and the water running to the lowest topographical spot in a stream.

Water is free-flowing and takes the shape of the container holding it. Therefore, water's shape is considered free-form. Because it falls to the lowest point, the color black and very deep, dark colors are associated with the water element.

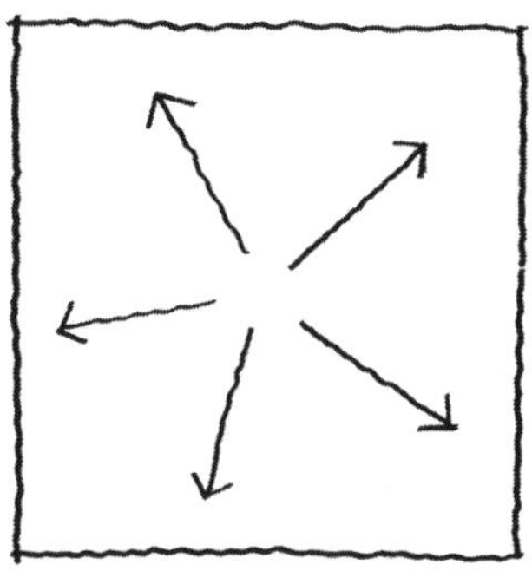

"Wood" energy is an expanding movement

Figure 22

Next, just like the tree in spring bursts forth with its new, expanding buds and opens them into flowers and leaves, the *expanding* energy is referred to as "wood." The columnar shape of a tree trunk, with its expanding rings, is also considered a wooden-shaped energy force. All shades of green are the colors of wood element.

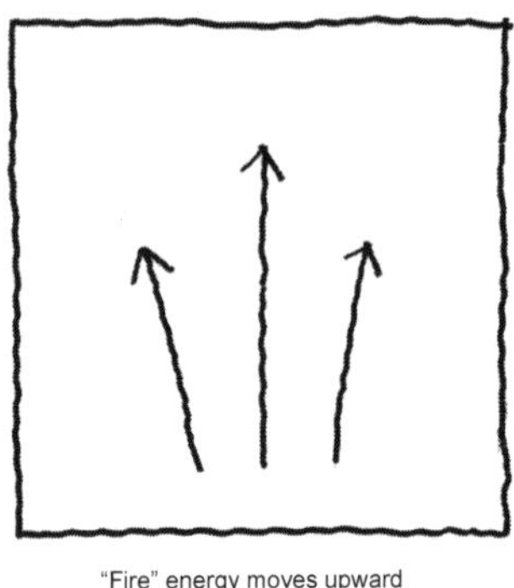

"Fire" energy moves upward

Figure 23

"Fire" is the name given to the *upward* force, as its movement copies how flames climb skyward. Triangular shapes are fire's mimicking shapes, and reds and fiery oranges are its colors.

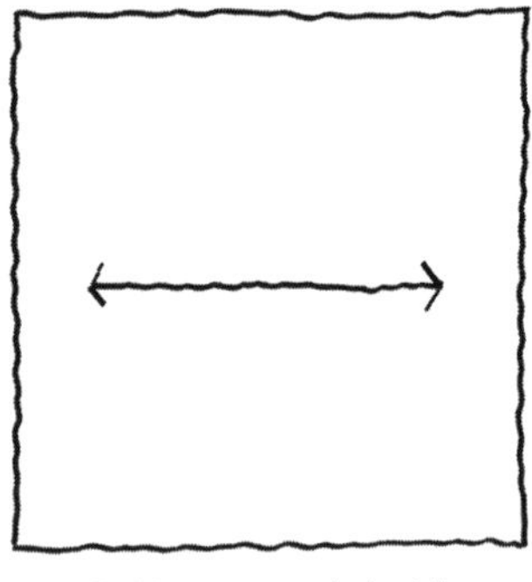

"Earth" energy moves horizontally

Figure 24

The *horizontal*, back-and-forth movement of energy is described as "earth" or soil, likening it to the movement along the surface of the ground. Flat or square shapes are considered to be earth element shapes, and earthy colors include yellows, browns, and earthy oranges.

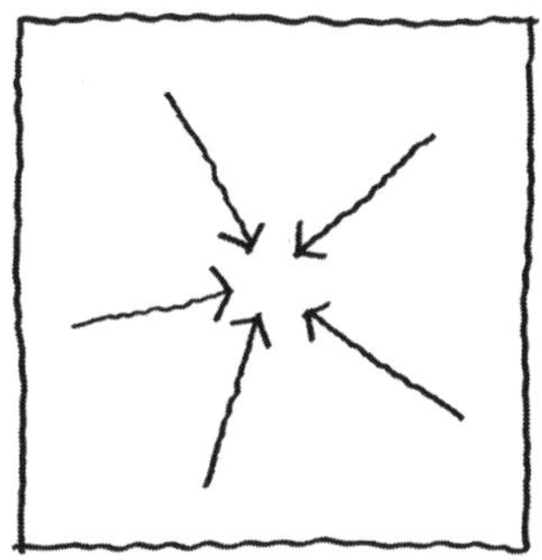

"Metal" energy movement is contracting/gathering

Figure 25

The "metal" element is associated with the compressing and *contracting* movement forces because of the inward-moving, "collecting" nature of these forces and the fact that they create tight spaces between molecules. (The earth compresses energy to create the metal within it.) Round shapes are considered metal element-oriented, as are white, metallic, and very light colors.

Remember, we're breaking down one thing—energy—into five stages. Sometimes the energy may be exhibiting clear signs of one specific element, and sometimes it may be "going" to the next element in the "circle of life," so it appears to be a mixture of two.

Everything, because it is a part of that one thing called energy, shows its five-element pattern if you know what to look for. Since we're talking about health and food, let's concentrate on those items within the body system. Here's a breakdown of all five elements with their associated body parts, organs, and tastes. (Yes, there actually is a taste associated with each element, even though when you see the food lists, you might not agree with the descriptions.) After that, you'll see some examples of foods in that element category and a description of who might be best served by eating them. (These lists are by no means comprehensive or complete. They are just to introduce the topic.)

Water Element

- Taste: Salty
- Organs: Kidneys and bladder
- Body parts: Low back and knees
- Values of water element people: Truth and spirituality
- Some water element foods: Fish, shellfish, pork, beans, seaweed, soy sauce, miso, walnuts, and black sesame seeds
- What water element foods do: Have a softening effect and promote moisture and calming of the body
- Who benefits most from water element foods: Thin, dry, and nervous people

Wood Element

- Taste: Sour
- Organs: Liver and gallbladder
- Body parts: Tendons and upper back
- Values of wood element people: Work and intensity
- Some wood element foods: Chicken, liver, wheat, greens, citrus fruits, plums, pineapple, vinegar, sauerkraut, olives, sourdough, and yogurt
- What wood element foods do: Function as astringents and help things run smoothly (blood, energy, emotions, etc.)
- Who benefits most from wood element foods: Angry, erratic, scattered people with low self-esteem

Fire Element

- Taste: Bitter

- Organs: Heart and small intestines
- Body parts: Eyes and hands
- Values of fire element people: Fun and variety
- Some fire element foods: Lamb, asparagus, lettuce, dandelion, alfalfa, celery, peppers, corn, cayenne, quinoa, oats, cumin, cherries, and peaches
- What fire element foods do: Reduce heat and dry fluids
- Who benefits most from fire element foods: Slow, overweight, overheated, and aggressive people

Earth Element

- Taste: Sweet
- Organs: Stomach and spleen
- Body parts: Muscles
- Values of earth element people: Helping, being of service, and stability
- Some earth element foods: Beef, millet, barley, rye, sugar, cooked onion, watermelon, apples, cherries, dates, figs, grapes, peaches, carrots, cabbage, potato, squash, almonds, and coconut
- What earth element foods do: Slow down acute symptoms and neutralize toxins
- Who benefits most from earth element foods: Dry, nervous, and weak people; these foods also calm aggression in people

Metal Element

- Taste: Spicy/Pungent
- Organs: Lungs and large intestines
- Body parts: Skin and hair
- Values of metal element people: Aesthetics, and the past and future
- Some metal element foods: Rice, raw onions, garlic, radish,

turnip, kohlrabi, cinnamon, mint, rosemary, scallions, cloves, fennel, anise, dill, mustard greens, horseradish, mustard, basil, and nutmeg

- What metal element foods do: Have a dispersing effect and promote energy circulation
- Who benefits most from metal element foods: Sluggish, damp, lethargic, and cold people

Here is a handy chart that includes much of the information covered so far above as well as a couple of bonus items that might be helpful.[12] Just like the five elements are "always going," please note that some foods fall into more than one category as well.

ELEMENT	WATER	WOOD	FIRE	EARTH	METAL
NEGATIVE EMOTION	Fear	Anger, Irritability	Sadness	Blame, Guilt, Worry	Depressed Outlook/Grief
POSITIVE EMOTION	Good Insights, Playfulness	Sense of Humor	Joy, Cheerful-ness	Empathy, Compassion	Positive Outlook
GRAIN	Buckwheat, Beans	Barley, Oats, Wheat	Corn	Millet	Rice, Quinoa, Amaranth
TASTE	Salty	Sour	Bitter	Sweet	Pungent/Spicy
SENSE IT CONTROLS	Hearing	Sight	Smell	Taste	Touch
YANG ORGAN	Bladder (Reproductive Organs)	Gallbladder	Small Intestine	Stomach	Large Intestine
YIN ORGAN	Kidneys	Liver	Heart	Spleen	Lungs
NATURE	Cold	Warm	Hot	Neutral	Cool
ENVIRONMENTAL CONDITIONS THAT TROUBLE IT	COLD, Dampness, Dryness	WIND, Heat, Dampness	HEAT, Dryness	DAMPNESS, Cold, Heat	DRYNESS, Heat, Cold, Phlegm

If you haven't already, write down the foods you eat most and see which element they are associated with and where they fall on this list. Then try to add a few helpful foods to your diet, or back off of unhelpful foods according to what you just read. And please continue your research on this subject—this is only the tip of the five-element food iceberg! If you're into feng shui, you probably already know that it's helpful to have all five elements represented in each room or space. It is the same with a meal. Optimally, you would have a representation of all five elements in food at each meal to create a balanced meal. Don't stress out about that—just keep it in mind when preparing meals or when you look back at what you ate to see if a simple tweak here and there would help.

The Bagua Balancer

> Whoever masters his emotions becomes a master of his life.

You know just how useless and time-wasting worrying really is *and* how it deteriorates your physical body. The same is true for other emotions, such as anger, guilt, fear, or sadness. But perhaps you're not sure you can pull off a five-element diet or are even having trouble with some Mind Modernizers that help free you from these unresourceful emotions. Don't worry. There's yet another way to balance the body's emotions. It uses the ancient feng shui map called the *bagua*.

The term *bagua* (pronounced ba-gwa) literally means "eight sides." Each individual section of the *bagua* is called a *gua* (pronounced gwa). The feng shui *bagua* map contains eight sections, or *guas*, that each relate to some element or energy in your life. With the *bagua* template, you can connect your living spaces with anything—and I mean ANYTHING—in your life. For this particular exercise, you are going to shift your physical space so that you can balance your emotional body.

Even though this Balancer could have just as easily been introduced in the Environmental Enhancing chapter, I wanted to place this feng shui strategy in Body Balancers to reiterate that FEELING a particular emotion is either going to be harmful, helpful, or possibly neutral to your health. I don't recommend allowing unwanted or negative feelings to continue to "plague you," as the repercussions can prove deadly.

Take the time now to note the specific unwanted emotions that seem to consistently plague you. You might want to use the same lists from previous strategies in this book or start a new, current list since your emotions may have shifted already. Some might have actually been around long enough to have given you their "down-line" physical diseases already, and some might be new.

This strategy uses the physical layout patterns in your living environments to shift your overall attitude, feelings, and emotions. I'd suggest working with this information in your bedroom first, then your office or daytime living space, and then anywhere else important where you spend time.

If you are familiar with the *bagua*, you'll pick this up in no time. For those who are new to the concept, consider this a new pattern that, if created in the rooms and buildings where you spend a lot of time, can not only support your emotional and physical health, but also literally help manifest the actual physical life circumstances that you have on your Dream Life list—such as a new job or a better relationship. Yeah! Three cheers for the *bagua* map!

First, take a look at the map, noting some of the negative feelings you are experiencing and some of the positive feelings that you would like to experience:

The *Bagua* Map of Emotions

When the **prosperity and abundance** *gua* is strong, you feel: grateful for your blessings, influencing, unbounded, proud, purposeful, cerebral, and resilient. When it is weak, you feel: your needs are not being met, you are bound, or the good life is elusive.	When the **fame and reputation** *gua* is working, you feel: passionate, piercing, blazing, "like a star," warm, friendly, engaging, intelligent, and shrewd. When it is not working, you feel: explosive, put out, unsupported, insecure, introverted, not respected, and lacking courage.	When the **relationship and love** *gua* is working, you feel: maternal, nurturing, accommodating, open, receptive, sheltering, and yielding. When it is not working, you feel: closed-hearted, non-accepting, inhumane, and indifferent.
When the **family** *gua* is supported, you feel: inventive, excited, swift, versatile, elastic, charming, stimulated, aroused, instigating, communicative, and "springy." When it is not working, you feel: stuck, still, unable to "get going," introverted, uninspired, and dependent.	When the **center** is working, you feel: healthy and vibrant. When it is not working, you feel: ill or physically weak.	When the **creativity and children** *gua* is working, you feel: joyous, playful, happy, creative, full of ideas, full of a sense of humor and wonder, and confident that you can get the job done. When it is not working, you feel: foolhardy, insensitive, defiant, arrogant, self-indulgent, anal retentive, controlling, or incapable of finishing things.
When the **skills and knowledge** *gua* is strong, you feel: self-assured, committed, firm, protective, calm, humble, responsible, and introspective. When it is not working, you feel: intimidated, confused, foggy, wishy-washy, undependable, and doubtful about your decisions.	When the **career** *gua* is working, you feel: "in the flow of life," adventurous, tactical, ingenious, adaptable, fearless, brave, and courageous. When it is not working, you feel: frustrated, confined, and downward spiraling.	When the **helpful people and travel** *gua* is working, you feel: efficient, prepared, predictable, and responded to. When it is not working, you feel: despotic, dispassionate, demanding, merciless, impassive, out of control, un-cared for, isolated, and as if you are doing everything yourself.

The door to the home, building, or room is ALWAYS along this bottom line of the *bagua* map.

The *bagua* map contains eight *guas* around "the center." I named each *gua* with its more traditional feng shui life circumstance-type name, such as "prosperity and abundance," "relationship and love," or "career." That way, not only can you connect the dots between other feng shui books and this chart, but you can also work specifically on that part of your life using this map, even if you do not identify with this *gua's* feelings.

The goal with this particular Balancer, though, is to help you to *feel better* so you can let the "law of attraction" work for you. But before we get into it, I'd like to reframe the "law of attraction" to give you what I think is a more accurate depiction of what is really going on, given everything you've read and tried from this book so far.

Instead of thinking that you somehow have to gussy up your energies to attract something that is "out there somewhere," consider this instead. Everything is one energy, and your consciousness is within it. So, there really is no "out there." It's all right here. So, how do you manifest it in your life? You release everything that is not it. That's the thoughts, the symbols in your environment, the clutter (space = opportunity, remember!), the unresourceful perceptions—ANYTHING that repels the energetic forces that you want near you.

Once you rid yourself of the untrue, "extra" negative emotions and other baggage that you've picked up along the way in life, you can GET BACK TO having positive and appropriate feelings and emotions. In other words, you don't have to hope that these feelings come your way. They are always there. They just sometimes get masked or shut out by the negative ones. And all you are required to do is strip the negative away.

Negative feelings and emotions literally block us from having what we want. They're like trees that fall across the road during a storm. The "good things" can't get through when there are roadblocks in the way. Using the *bagua* map, like some of the previous Mind Modernizers, helps us remove the negative feelings so our desires can continue heading right toward us—and so our life syncs up with our dreams.

Using the *Bagua* Map

Begin by standing in your bedroom door looking in with the map in front of you. You are walking into either the Skills and Knowledge *gua*, the Career *gua*, or the Helpful People and Travel *gua*—depending on whether the door is on the left side of the room, in the center, or on the right. If your bedroom's layout is unusual or confusing for some reason, simply stand at the bottom of your bed (consider that the door) and overlay the map onto your bed instead of your room. In doing this, you're really employing the rule "what's closest to you has the most impact on you." Or, if you wish, you can go to another room where you spend a lot of time and practice there.

If you've got your map correctly laid out, the Prosperity and Abundance *gua* is farthest from you on the left, and the Relationships and Love *gua* is back on the right. Take a look at what is in each "one-ninth" of the room to see if there is any glaring connection between the stuff that is there and how you feel or what is going on in your life. For example, many "single-and-constantly-looking" people have pictures of themselves alone in a frame in the relationship *gua*. Or perhaps there is a big pile of clutter in the Prosperity and Abundance *gua* taking up all the "opportunity space" for prosperity in your life. You won't believe how often your stuff literally describes your life. Of course, if you read *Move Your Stuff, Change Your Life*, you probably remember that "the villain" of the book was the toilet, because so many people who suffered financial loss had toilets in their Prosperity and Abundance *guas*. Do your toilet locations and your negative life circumstances connect?

Step one is to remove anything that you see as a negative connotation affecting that area of your life, but "permanent" things like toilets probably need to be cured instead. Close the door and keep the lid down for sure, and if you need to, add the "mirror facing out" on the door to deflect healthy energy from entering the bathroom to be drained away. Or, be more subtle by running a line of red color across the top moulding of the door with intentions of stopping the energy from crossing the line to mitigate the situation.

Now, if you want to add something, consider adding something that you feel would positively promote that aspect of your life in this particular area of the room. For example, you could place an item that makes you feel abundant in the back left, or something that feels romantic to you in the back right.

Remember the rule, "It does not have to be seen to be effective." Hide your helpful items if they don't fit the décor or suit your taste.

Here's a list of helpful and harmful items for each *gua*:

Prosperity and Abundance *Gua*

Helpful: Plants; mirrors; columnar shapes; purple, green, or black colors; pictures with moving water and/or trees in them; actual water (but I would not recommend placing a fountain or an aquarium in your bedroom); or any symbols that remind you of being abundant or that make you feel any of the positive feelings you see in the prosperity and abundance part of the *bagua* map of emotions.

Harmful: White colors, metallic objects, fiery items (candles, a fireplace, images of the sun or stars), fiery colors, broken items, dirty stuff, and clutter.

Fame and Reputation *Gua*

Helpful: Fiery stuff like fireplaces and candles, plants and trees, reds and hot orange colors, leather, animal print fabrics, pointy or triangular-shaped items, or any symbols or items that would make you feel or remind you of the positive emotions from that part of the map. For example, you might simply have the word "passionate" written somewhere in this part of the room.

Harmful: Water, mirrors, art with moving water in it, black and very dark colors, earthy stuff like pottery, sand, or dirt—and of course, clutter.

Relationships and Love *Gua*

Helpful: Earthy items like stones, pottery, and ceramics; pictures with mountains or earth in them; earth tones and pink colors; matching pairs of items; romantic/sensual-feeling items; symbols of love and good relationships; symbols or items that support you feeling the positive emotions on the *bagua* map above for this *gua*.

Harmful: Single objects and people alone in pictures, trees and wooden items, green colors, cold symbols (like pictures with snow in them or an actual freezer), distractions from romance (like work- or workout-related items, hobbies, etc.), and of course, good ol' clutter.

Creativity and Children *Gua*

Helpful: Metallic or earthy items; anything made of metal; round, mounded, or square object shapes; white, pastel, metallic, earthy, or yellow colors; symbols of fun, joy, or creativity or any of the positive emotions associated with this *gua*; and pictures of children or anything that makes you laugh.

Harmful: Items that "bring you down," fiery stuff like candles and red or hot colors, animal print or leather stuff, water, black and dark colors, mirrors, and—you guessed it—clutter.

Helpful People and Travel *Gua*

Helpful: Metallic or earthy items; anything made of metal; round, mounded, or square object shapes; white, pastel, metallic, earthy, or yellow colors; maps or items that remind you of places you wish to go in the world; and anything that makes you feel efficient or any other positive emotion from the map. This is the location where you would place your Helpful People Modernizer Box.

Harmful: Fiery stuff like candles and red or hot colors, animal print or leather stuff, water, black and dark colors, mirrors, symbols of places you do not wish to visit or travel to, and to no one's surprise: clutter.

Career and Life Path *Gua*

Helpful: Water, mirrors, undulating or free-form shaped items, black or dark colors, metallic or round-shaped items, symbols with moving water in them, symbols of what you want to do in life (career, hobby, or otherwise), and symbols that make you feel the positive emotions from this section of the map.

Harmful: Earthy items and colors; yellow; square shapes; trees, plants, and wooden items; columnar shapes; symbols of what you don't want to do—I had a client who had a picture of a guy walking a tight rope in this part of his home, and he said that was how he felt all the time in life—and clutter once again.

Skills and Knowledge *Gua*

Helpful: Earthy items and colors, yellows and blues, square shapes, light, symbols of wisdom or wise beings, symbols of any of the other positive emotions on the map, books, or any other self-cultivation items.

Harmful: Clutter of course, columnar shaped items, green colors, tree-shaped plants, clutter, alcohol, drugs, junk food or other substances that dull the senses or do not support the body, or any item that makes you feel the negative emotions on the Bagua Map.

Family *Gua*

Helpful: Wooden things, green colors, columnar-shaped items, pictures of ancestors and family members, water and mirrors and free-form shapes, and symbols of good relationships within the family or any of the positive emotions in this part of the map.

Harmful: Metallic stuff; white, metallic and pastel colors; fire items and symbols; red and hot colors; round or triangular shapes; and—do I need to say it?—clutter.

The Center

Helpful: Earthy items and colors, yellow items and colors, pictures depicting mountains and earthy things, square-shaped items, flat surfaces, and any symbol that makes you feel healthier—perhaps it is a symbol or picture of a healthy body part that needs healing on your body. (I use medical book illustrations of healthy internal body parts.)

Harmful: Trees and wooden items, green colors, metallic items and colors (white and pastels), unhealthy items (like alcohol or junk food), unhealthy symbols, and clutter.

Now, there's no need to get crazy by clearing out ALL of the harmful items and overloading the good stuff there. The goal is to find a balance and to get the positive emotions to start to show up more than the negative, eventually wiping away the negative ones. If it makes no sense to remove the negative things (like, that is the only place for the freezer!), organize the space in a way that works functionally for you and also somehow has the helpful items above be more dominant than the negative things. And don't forget the rule that it doesn't have to be seen to work. I hide little symbols behind pictures and in drawers all the time!

You might need to experiment by changing some things and seeing what the result is in your life. I'd say it would take no more than six weeks to know (it can, however, happen immediately or overnight). The more mindful you are about your environment in this way, the more you can fine tune your life and your emotions using the *bagua* map.

The Cooking Balancer

I know we've already discussed how the stove works best for prosperity and respect-building if it is in the armchair position and is clean and everything is working, but now it is time to discuss the stove from a physical, health-generating, feng shui perspective, since it is usually an integral item with regard to food preparation.

Any feng shui expert would say that cooking over open flames is "the best way to cook." (Go campers!) It is certainly the most natural, wouldn't you agree? But many modern, Western homes don't have the open fire option.

So, let's talk about the contemporary cooking options.

Of the stove and "cooker" choices, the gas stove (well-ventilated, of course) is the next healthiest option to an actual fire, as it has actual "fire-element" flames like the wood-burning fire does. The electric stoves would fall behind open fire and gas stoves in this regard. Now, we're getting into a pretty unnatural environment of cooking on top of an electrical heat source.

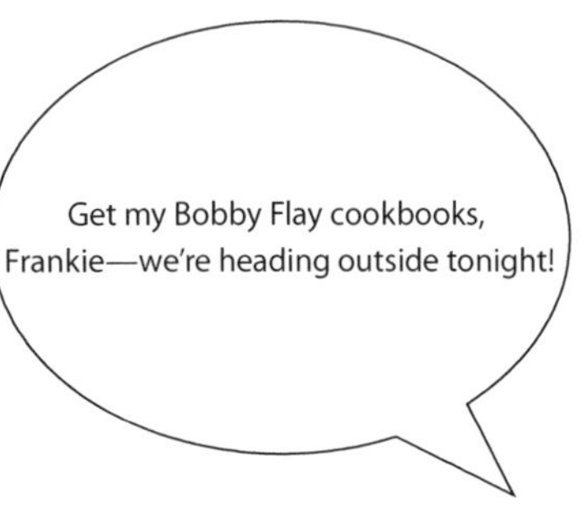

So, we've got open fire, then gas, and then electric stoves and ovens for our cooking lineup. Where's the microwave, you ask? Well, if you skimmed over that topic in the Ambient Energy Enhancer in Chapter 3, let me clarify: consider it "not an option." Not only is the food in a microwave heated from the inside out, literally scrambling the molecules to a point where the friction between them causes heat (not natural to say the least), but you get the added negative bonus of leaking microwave **radiation** in your house (and into you) as you stand near it while it's heating your food.

If you are freaking out right now with thoughts of "I can't LIVE without my microwave," I'd like to rebut, "You can't live WITH your microwave." But if you want real practical advice, here you go. Get a pan and put food in it. Put the pan and food on top of a stove burner. Turn on the stove burner. Or place food on a stoneware plate and heat it in the oven on a low temperature. Problem solved. Popcorn pops, butter melts, coffee or tea water heats nicely, and leftovers get hot. There are also insulated food storage thermoses to use if you want to heat a frozen meal in the oven and take it to work for lunch. Some brands keep food hot for seven hours.

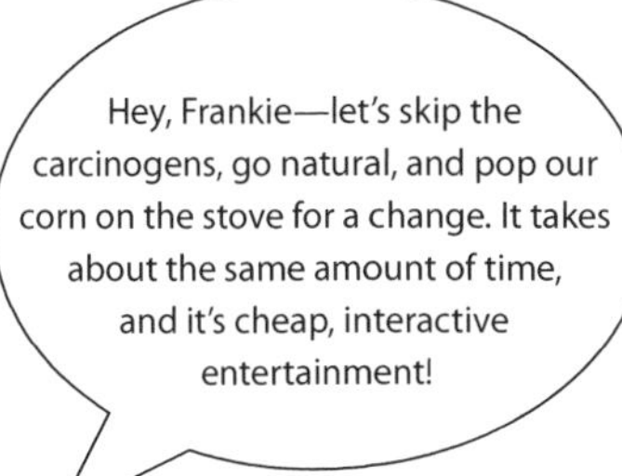

Let me tell you a little story from one of my consultations to give you a sense of what I believe to be the results of repeated microwave eating and overexposure to electromagnetic fields. I went to a home where the parents had two boys. At the time, the brothers were about three and six years old. Both kids had SEVERE language issues as well as other ailments like allergies, etc. Now when I say "severe," I mean they couldn't even keep their own name and their brother's name straight. Have you ever seen a kid ask, "Where's Bobby?" and the mother reply saying, "Honey, you're Bobby. And your brother Nate is with Daddy." That's severe. It appeared that their brains were somehow "scrambled."

The mother confessed that each and every (plastic) baby bottle that they had ever been given, and each and every hot meal they had eaten had been microwaved. I personally don't EVER want to see the look on a mother's face like that again, so I'm telling you all now, avoid the microwave—and for God's sake, ESPECIALLY if you are putting plastic in there with your food!

In this mom's defense, besides suffering from the lack of nutrition going into their bodies, her kids were in extremely poor bed positions (in line with the door and not in the armchair position), and those beds were located in extremely strong electromagnetic fields, so it may have been the combination of those factors that brought on these drastic results. (Why don't doctors regularly consider the environmental exposures when treating their patients?)

I raised this point in Chapter 3, but it bears repeating here: you know better than to put your head in the microwave and turn it on, right? Well then, why is it OK to heat food in the microwave and then put THAT hot food into your head to feed your body? No thanks.

Using the microwave is really just a habit. And this habit has very good and simple alternatives.

The Sleep Balancer

Right up there with water and food, sleep is obviously vital for a healthy body. It is also very closely connected to relationships and relationship-building, if you've never connected the dots on that before.

I can't tell you how many of my clients have said that I "saved their life," both health- and relationship-wise, after they implemented the suggestions I made regarding sleep. Some clients didn't really even know they were *not* getting enough sleep until they got some quality shut-eye, they were so used to feeling sleep deprived.

When I was in college, I ran so consistently sleep-deprived that I started to think of sleeping every night as a waste of time—even though I literally fell asleep walking and started hallucinating once! I was in the habit of only sleeping every third night for almost a whole semester, one time even going totally sleepless for five days (the hallucinating time mentioned above). That's messed up! So, I've been there, and I know how mentally unsettling and unbalancing it can be.

Here are some signs sleep-deprived people usually show but don't connect to lack of sleep. Can you relate to any of these?

1. You have trouble with spatial relationship tasks, like de-cluttering and organizing, for example.
2. You think or have been told by others that you have a drinking problem.
3. You have been told that you snore or hold your breath while you sleep, or you have been diagnosed with sleep apnea.
4. You fall asleep while sitting up rather quickly after sitting down or even driving.

5. Your mind does not want to "turn off" at night, and you find yourself having trouble falling or staying asleep.
6. You consistently feel anxious or like you can't handle stress—quite often not even knowing exactly what you are anxious over.
7. You have poor memory, concentration, and decision-making—even risky behavior—and possibly other mental health issues.
8. You have depression, burnout, decreased empathy, mood swings, vision and motor skills issues, high blood pressure, weakened immune function, and the various associated medical issues that arise from immune deficiency.
9. Your appetite is increased. (There is clear evidence of a link between obesity and lack of sleep.)
10. You have multiple accidents or consider yourself clumsy.
11. You've been assigned the couch or other sleeping space by your partner, or your partner has bugged out due to your sleep deprivation issues.

Now that I probably have your attention, here are a few suggestions:

Investigate environmental and other changes that have occurred since the time you did sleep well. What are the differences in yourself, your habits, or your environment that have occurred between the time when you last slept well and now? Did you exercise more then? Did you consume less caffeine then? Did you (or a neighbor) add a wireless transmitter in your home? (If your neighbor's Wi-Fi signal is noticed on your computer, you are in their wireless field.) Did you start charging your cell phone at night next to your bed? Did you paint the room a different color? Did you change your bedding to more synthetic materials? Did you have a baby? Do you have a pesticide service coming now that you didn't have then? Did you start or stop taking a drug or herbs? Have you stopped a relaxing hobby or your meditation practice? Did you get divorced, and are you now sleeping alone? Did your spouse start snoring? Pinpointing the nuances that contribute to good sleep and bad sleep can potentially mean simple changes if you think this way. (All of the above and then some can be contributing factors.) Once again, work the trial and error method—make one of the following changes and see if it improves your sleep. If not, then move on to the next one.

1. Track your sleep and see if your waking hours run consistent with the moon cycles. If so, you will probably notice less sound sleep when the moon is fuller.
2. Avoid caffeine and other "yang" substances like recreational drugs, alcohol, nicotine, and excessive sugar or carbs. Sleeping is connected to more yin attributes. Even simply exchanging your bedtime sweet snack (yang) to a salty one (yin) could help—get it?
3. Experiment by turning off all the electricity in the home before retiring to bed. You may just be reacting to your electrically "hopped-up" house. (Don't worry, the food stays cold enough in the fridge overnight.) If your ability to sleep improves, each night turn on another breaker, and see if that particular breaker's worth of electrical circuitry seems to negatively affect your sleep.

   Keep turning on more and more breakers, or swap them around off and on systematically until you figure out which ones can be on, and in what combination, without affecting your sleep. This is a trial and error-type method for sure, but one that you can do for free and on your own. (Unfortunately, if you rent, you probably have adjacent tenant spaces that you have no control over.) I would also suggest removing the television from the room if it is still in there.

If you have control over your space, and you indeed saw considerable improvement by cutting off electricity at certain breakers (usually in your bedroom), consider hiring an electrician to install a "demand switch" for the bedroom. A demand switch gives you the ability to turn off and on the electricity to the whole room right in the room as opposed to having to go to the breaker box/circuit panel, so you have easy access to and control over the electrical fields and electromagnetic fields surrounding you at night.

4. If you can't "turn your brain off" at night, try this home-remedy: soak your feet in warm water before retiring to bed. This pulls your energy downward and out of your head.
5. A traditional feng shui cure for temporary insomnia is to place a stone on the floor near the head of the bed to add the energy of stillness ("to sleep like a rock") for a number of nights (9, 18, or 27).
6. If you always find yourself rehashing the past instead of being in the present moment, remove any mirrors that are on walls that are consistently behind you where you spend a lot of time, such as the headboard wall in your bedroom or behind your desk. It may be the case that the offending mirror is simply on the back wall of the house.
7. Block out noises by hanging a wind chime between your bed and the offending noise. The chime can be hung all the way out along your property line if the noise is located off of your property.
8. If none of these changes works, you might consider seeing a Traditional Chinese Medicine practitioner, a doctor, or a feng shui consultant (or all three!) to see if there is anything else they can see that you are missing.

The Grounding Balancer

If you paid attention to Chapter 3's Ambient Energy Enhancer and the prior Sleep Balancer, you should have already removed as many electrically charged items from your sleep and daytime living spaces as possible, and you may already be experiencing less stress, reduced pain, and a better night's sleep. But there is something else that can be done to further help rest, repair, and revive our bodies, and that is grounding. Grounding is literally contacting your skin to the earth so that the earth's electrons can neutralize your positively charged body.

When you contact the earth like this, you literally become grounded like any other electrical device that plugs into a socket with a grounding prong, resulting in a neutrally charged body. When the body is not holding a charge, you are much more likely to sleep better and have less chronic pain.

I would recommend grounding yourself for 30 minutes each day. Do not discount this simple, low- or no-cost solution. It may be just what you've been looking for! What have you got to lose besides an unhealthy positive charge on your body?

If you don't have the weather for spending barefooted time outdoors, or just plain old don't have the time, there are grounding items (sheets and grounding pads, etc.) available for purchase that can be placed on your bed or underfoot while you are sitting at your desk.[13] There are even ones that you attach to yourself while plugging the other end of the cord into the grounding wire in your house, so there's really no excuse not to take advantage of this Balancer. And honestly, it could be just the ticket to your health—especially as we live in a more and more electrically polluted environment.

Grounding Healing Meditation

As long as you are standing there grounding yourself, spend your time wisely and do this three-part healing meditation/visualization traditionally called the Great Sunshine Buddha Meditation. This practice was taught to me by my feng shui master, the late Grand Master Lin Yun.

Stand with your feet shoulders' width apart and tilt your head up toward the sun. (This also can be done indoors as a simple healing meditation if you can't get outdoors. You just visualize the sun above you.)

Part 1: Raise your arms and place your hands, palms up, above your head. Visualize that the sun's rays are entering your forehead (third eye chakra) and palms and that the sun's energy is traveling down inside your entire body to your feet. Place your arms down at your side.

Part 2: Raise your palms back up into the above-the-head, palms-up position again. Visualize the sun's energy coming in through your third eye and your palms and moving down the body as before. Then have it bounce at the bottom of your feet and go quickly back up and out the head and palms where it came in. Lower your hands to your sides.

Part 3: Raise your hands back up again as before, and bring the energy in as before. Once it touches the bottom of your feet, picture the energy as two small suns (it will warm up your feet!) which will then slowly start to spiral up throughout your body. As the energy spirals up, visualize it removing all of your aches, pains, sick cells, or any other unhealthy items from your body as it exits out of your hands and head. After the energy has left your body, visualize your body as fully healthy and glowing.

Repeat the sequence nine times. The traditional method of this healing meditation is to perform it nine times a day for 27 days.

The Moving Balancer

If you are weak, eat something strong (like ginseng that grows into rock!). If you can't hop out of bed in the morning, eat rabbit. If you don't want to be a couch potato, stop eating potatoes. If life is moving too fast, stop eating things that have travelled 70 miles an hour in a truck after just getting off a 20-mile-an-hour conveyor belt!

The whole game here is mindfulness. Everything is energy, and it is good to remind yourself of what kind of energy you need to perform as efficiently as possible. So, with your air, water, food, and emotions considered, there's one last thing to consider that can shift your body toward balance and health, and that is how much you move.

Become mindful of how much you move during the day. Then modify your efforts according to the results you wish to achieve. Some of you may find that things like yoga and *Tai Chi* are right for you and that high impact cardio at the gym isn't.

Remember my client Cathie, who needed two new knees and had to lose over 100 pounds? She decided (it starts in the mind!) that working out in a gym and learning how to kayak were for her, although she had absolutely no prior experience with either.

Years ago, back before I was ever into feng shui when I was running my landscape architecture firm, I had the foresight to try to "balance myself" with *Tai Chi* because I felt that I was just "going too fast." Everything was in a rush, and I felt very impatient and flustered for days on end. I chose *Tai Chi* because somehow, without knowing too much about it (I hate to admit this, but this was before the Internet), I thought, "the more slowly you do it, the better it is."

I had learned all 64 postures when my teacher decided to teach us "slow form." This is where you take one of the 64 postures and do it in the same amount of time you normally take to do all 64 postures—around 30 to 40 minutes.

My immediate reaction was, "Oh my God, that sounds horrific!

How boring, blah, blah, blah . . . ." (Yep, I was still a newbie grasshopper.) But once we started doing it, I LOVED IT! It became my favorite form of *Tai Chi*. It is a true moving meditation. You literally feel and are aware of each and every ligament and muscle firing and moving. It was remarkable to notice what all was going on as I was moving so slooooooooooow. We moved so slowly, it was virtually unperceivable.

What environmental changes could you make to manifest a possible new type of movement in your life? What mind-shifters have to take place to actually get you to believe that it is possible, you are capable, and you deserve to do it? What prosperity *gua* enhancements do you need to apply to generate the funds that would support your new dream movement? How can you support your body to actually thrive during the "exercises" you choose? Imagine it, believe it, build the space for it, and then "just do it!"

You CAN do it!

The WooWoo Balancer

I added this Balancer for those who have never thought outside the "Western medicine paradigm" box as a possibility for maintaining or regaining health. There are countless valuable alternative treatments and therapies that you may not ever hear about if you only listen to your traditionally trained doctor (although more and more, western-trained doctors are looking outside their boxes for better treatment ideas).

Although some of these alternative modalities are new, many predate Western medicine and are more commonly used in much healthier countries than the US. I'm not here to tell you to drop your existing doctors or the treatments they are prescribing; I am only asking you to think of them like your employees and monitor their results. In other words, don't believe that their approach is the only way to go. Consider alternative treatments if you've done all you can do working through this book and you still find yourself unhealthy or suffering—or if you have been given a life sentence of meds, with no plan or possibility of getting off of them to deal with the pain or other symptoms.

By the way, if the thought of getting off of your medications scares you, or if you believe that anything besides Western medicine is "a sham," perhaps you have been given a mind virus that needs extraction with some of the Mind Modernizers.

You might also want to place the names of everyone associated with your health (doctors, insurance companies, alternative treatment practitioners, etc.) in your Helpful People Box, with the intention of making sure they are ALWAYS helpful to you and your consistent state of health.

Considering alternative treatments is not really that "woowoo" anymore!

Chapter 5: Serve Your Spirit

What are the benefits of serving your spirit? Among others, some prime benefits are living, being, and feeling whole. Wholeness includes your mind, body, and environment—as well as your spirit.

"Doesn't living a spiritual life have to be boring?" you might ask. Or, "doesn't it require you to be poor?" The answer is: not unless you choose to believe that it does. The truth is: the experience of living a spiritual life can reflect anything you choose to believe about it. This being the case, why not choose a belief that empowers you?

Another question that might arise concerns the relationship between spirituality and religion. "Does this type of stuff mess with my religion?" you might wonder. It can and will if you choose to take on that thought or belief, but by now I suspect you are on to how thoughts like that limit you. Spirituality is a more encompassing concept that incorporates religion, in much the same way as the ocean incorporates waves. Forces in the ocean can affect the flow of waves, but at the same time, waves are an expression of the ocean. The two are inextricably intertwined. So, too, are spirituality and religion.

The word *religion* actually comes from the word *Deena* in Aramaic, which means "balance or harmony." If the concept of religion has its deeper roots in balance and harmony, then everything in this book has a religious bent to it, in a sense. It is *all* designed to produce harmony, balance, and wholeness in every aspect of your life. (If this notion is putting you into a negative head-spin, return to the Mind Modernizers to push past prior programming that might be holding you back.)

When you acknowledge and maintain your access to your spirit, you align yourself with your divine flow—much like Providence, which we've already been working with. This alignment can change your life's results and outcomes in a snap. Your health, happiness, abundance, or anything else on that Dream Life list can be just as easily "worked" by serving your spirit as well as by any of the other means we've discussed. So why, then, doesn't everybody constantly strive to serve their spirit? My guess is that there is a chronic compulsion to DO something in the visible realm before "trusting" in the invisible or spiritual realm.

Indeed, I saved the Spirit Servers for last because of the very fact that most people want to DO things to shift their lives in a better direction. "*Being* your way to happiness" seems so, well . . . flimsy, or weak. And so, by sharing the mind, environment, and body enhancing strategies first, my hope was to make it clear that, if you want, there is stuff you can "do."

But the one thing that many people forget is that we are not human doings. We are human beings. And when you shift to BEING and release all the doing, you are actually more closely aligned with the energies of your true nature. This alignment connects you to the flow of life that brings an unceasing inner peace, freedom, and sense of contentment—which are probably the end result feelings of every item on your Dream List.

The focus of our discussion here is the "already always eternalness of spirit that is outside of time." It stands in contrast to the "always fleetingness of all things that are within time." If you can clear away all of the in-time "doing to get" and allow the already always spirit to simply be, you will notice that list that you wrote in the beginning of this book effortlessly unfolding rather than emerging as a hard-fought result of all your doing.

So, what was the point of all of the "doing" techniques presented earlier? *It is easier for surrender to happen after everything else has already been tried.* No ego in its right mind wants to give up the unlimited array of things to do and simply be, just because someone—or worse yet, some book—says to do so. The ego simply feels it MUST DO something, usually in the 3-D, physical world. The ego's very existence is based upon the constant worldly distractions of life itself. But indeed, it is that ego that must be tamed to allow the powerful universal energy to flow within you.

All of the "doing" work we did was certainly not useless. It was actually the preparation necessary for living a high-vibrating life. Consider the moment of surrendering, after all that prep work, as the first step of your spiritual journey. Athletes don't train once and then race forever. They will DO the same training techniques for each subsequent race as they did for the first, fine tuning their practice along the way because of lessons learned. So trust me, those mind, environment, and body shifters will continue to come in handy. But these Spirit Servers, because they link up to very "well-established" or "seasoned" energies, if you will, can be the most powerful tactics of all.

Depending on your vibration level, these Spirit Servers may seem anything from basic, to appropriate, to overwhelming or even impossible. But you've got the techniques now to move you past unresourceful thoughts and keep you going. So, without further ado, here are my favorite Spirit Servers that really help me and my clients get our shift together!

The Intending and Invoking Server

It might seem like we're splitting hairs, but if you can make the distinction between "intending or invoking" and "wanting or inviting," you will be able to harness helpful energies that much faster with many of the techniques throughout this book.

The word *intend* comes from root words meaning "to stretch out" and "to plan." The word *invoke* comes from root words meaning "to give voice to" or "to call." The root of the word *invite*, on the other hand, is "to seek." Based on these meanings, there is more power involved when you invoke than when you invite. When you invoke, you assume not only that the heavenly energies are listening, but also that they are immediately available to take part or help you achieve your outcome now.

Take a look at two different ways to set an intention of healing the planet. The first way is simple, straightforward, and clear: "I invoke the all-powerful energies to restore ecological harmony to the planet now." This statement is a declaration; it serves to "summon up" those universal energies with a direct command. By contrast, an invitation-type statement might sound like this: "If you are listening, I invite all of you out there to come and make the world a better place." This invitation has a different feel to it than the invocation, does it not? Hmmm . . . like, maybe they will and maybe they won't help the planet.

Another area where we might compare invoking versus inviting statements concerns prayers for healing. Many people pray like this: "Please heal me." This is framed as an invitation or as a request. The vibration that this prayer is expressing is actually the following: "I would like to have your help with my healing, and I invite you to give it." By far a more powerful way to go is similar to the intention that a charismatic healer invokes. They firmly command, "HEAL!" or "Be healed!" They are not requesting or inviting help; they are assuming that you WILL BE healed.

So, when planning a shift toward your Dream Life, align your spiritual forces by having clear intentions regarding what you want. Then invoke the invisible, energetic, spiritual resources that assist you to "handle it."

One tip that I learned as a feng shui initiate was to visualize my teachers standing behind me looking over my shoulders as I set my intentions and invoked the invisible energies forward on my client's behalf. Even if you can't hold your intentions very strongly, your teachers can hold them for you or with you.

Here's a to-do list for Intending and Invoking:

1. Stand or sit up straight, with your feet firmly planted on the ground. Good posture and invoking are connected.
2. Tap the top of your head to ignite the crown of your head to consciously "plug in" to the universal energy above.
3. Get a solemn and clear picture in your mind of what you are intending. Then state it in words, either mentally or out loud.
4. With a commanding tone (as opposed to a begging or groveling one), state "I decree or I invoke . . . " and continue stating your intention. Avoid "inviting-type" beginnings to your statements, such as "I wish, I want, or I invite . . . ."
5. Feel the inner physical body shifts.
6. Be in gratitude.

When is it appropriate to use this Spirit Server? The answer is: anytime. By invoking in this manner, you WILL service your spirit by simply acknowledging it. It's like ringing a doorbell. You will attract and get attention from your spiritual source and the universal energies that assist you.

Here are some examples of invoking statements you might use to achieve different intentions:

- **For expanding your thinking**—"I invoke the heavenly energies to support me in clearing my negative thoughts and beliefs!"
- **For improving your health**—"I invoke all heavenly support for my full and complete recovery now."
- **For overall well-being**—"I invoke that the Universe is constantly conspiring to make me happy."

Experiment with other statements as you put the Intending and Invoking Server to work for you.

The Creativity Server

What do opera divas, comedians, writers, and whirling dervishes all have in common? They have allowed their bodies to be infused with spirit to bring forth a unique display of energy called creativity.

Creativity is spirit manifesting itself. It is a way of moving the accumulated energy you have acquired from using all of the other processes in this book. If you keep the energy moving, it does not congest, causing you feelings of stuck-ness or burnout. Optimally, you would be best served if you accumulate it, transform it (up-leveling), and express it in some creative capacity.

Being a creator is as close to *being* universal energy, Source, God-like, Buddha-minded, or _______________ (insert your favorite enlightenment word here) as you can get. The very definition of *creator* includes concepts such as "originator, initiator, founder, designer, prime mover, Supreme Being, the Deity, and God." So, if you want to align with the oneness of the universe, create!

You may have a story in your head about not being creative. If so, zap it with the Energy Transfer Modernizer: it is possible for you to be creative now; you are capable of being creative now; and you deserve to be creative now. Or, if you want to skip the Modernizer and move on, try reframing your thoughts on what counts as "creative." You literally "create" your day every day by the options you choose. Because you *make* choices in every moment, you actually can't avoid constantly creating.

How to Serve Your Creativity

If you are completely stumped and still feel lost with regard to conscious creativity, use other helpful tools from this book. Start writing about it, Dream Diary Modernizer-style. Dream out on paper what creativity looks like and how it feels first, and then let it take form in whatever way shows up. If you can, block out or *create* a physical space for creativity in your home using the "If You Build It" Environmental Enhancer technique.

If you feel creative but want an added boost, practice *satori*, which is catching yourself and becoming aware of yourself while in the midst of "doing" something creative.

The Sitting in Silence Server

In this world of e-mails, texts, apps, and the like, it's all you can do to stop and take a breath, let alone sit quietly and contemplate or meditate. Our fascination with all things "of this world" has us focusing on everything but our connection to our true nature as Spirit. (Once again, feel free to insert the cultural word for "Spirit" that suits you.)

> If everyone could only experience what there is to gain before meditating or "sitting in silence," there would be more people willing to put some effort into it.

Meditation, or "sitting in silence," is about "stopping the noise" of the illusory "me, myself, and I" egoic world so you can *re-cognize* and *re-connect* with the timeless higher-vibrating realms and *re-member* that you are not ever alone. When you have this connection, you literally drop all judgments and any meanings that you have assigned to all things worldly, because your attention is "elsewhere." And since energy follows thought, literally ALL of your feelings—for better or worse—"go into neutral," if they are there at all. It is THAT PLACE where those high-vibrating "feelings" like joy, peace, bliss, and enlightenment (a.k.a. "heaven") exist. The kingdom of heaven is truly within.

Also, when you meditate consistently, you have the ability to uplift your worldly life significantly as well, because you then have:

- The ability to focus (better);
- The ability to adapt to life circumstances (better);
- The ability to deepen your senses and trust your "sixth sense" (better);
- The ability to observe situations with multiple viewpoints, and usually distill them to their most simple state, reaching deeper and multi-faceted conclusions about them; and
- The ability to understand, gain wisdom, and attain "inspiration" for your goals and projects.

Although this process may not be easy, there is not a more simple process in this book than this one. To sit in silence is to release (what you perceive as) "your control" and make contact with very high-vibrating energy. When you contact with this level of energy, you are at an advantage when life tests you with its challenges. As a matter of fact, with this better advantage, crisis-type challenges (a.k.a. spirit trainings) of the past are now seen as interesting obstacles to watch yourself react to, or mere curiosities, if they are still seen as challenges at all.

So, how do you make the time and take the time to actually sit and "do" nothing?

First of all, to make the time, I recommend finding a consistent time each day. Perhaps it is the first thing you do in the morning, or the last thing before retiring, or maybe you prefer a few moments just before you have to get in the car to pick up the kids. Experiment and see what works best for you.

When I started meditating (back in my "I hear dead people" days—now THERE's motivation!), I sat for one hour each day before leaving for work. I had the house to myself then, and I noticed it gave me the perfect attitude adjustment before heading into my usual full work day. If you don't have one hour, start with thirty minutes, or three minutes—whatever you've got. Just stay consistent until it becomes a habit and you feel like you are missing something if you don't do it.

Next, while considering the perfect time for you, choose a location and create a meditation-conducive physical environment. Remember, if you build it, you will come and sit down!

Build the space with the following criteria, and you're off to a good start:

1. It should be devoid of electrical and wireless devices.
2. It would be best if it were in a location where sudden disturbances (someone talking to you, a loud noise, a phone ringing) would not occur.
3. It should be comfortable enough to promote relaxation, but not sleep. If you are totally new to sitting in silence, I would recommend sitting in a straight-backed chair. Experiment with what you like. I tried chair after chair until I settled on the one I use now.
4. It would be better if the space was more yin than yang—meaning smaller, cozier, darker, etc. Most people find it easier to do this in a small space rather than a wide open one. I'm not sure if it's why monks do it, but I find it a whole lot easier to sit still and focus when I have a hood up and over my head, as it feels like the "space" I'm in is much smaller.
5. It might be better if you have a lit candle nearby. The flame is a symbol of transformation as well as focus.

My space is literally in my walk-in dressing room. There is no reason for anyone to be in there but me, so I know I won't be interrupted. I have my chair, a rug, my iPod, candles, and matches all ready to go.

With the time carved out and the physical space ready for use, give it a try.

1. Light a candle with the intention of meditating.
2. Sit in your chair with feet firmly grounded on the floor.

3. Get comfortable, but preferably with your spine off the back of the chair (if your spine is aligned, you can sit in a relaxed position without having to hold yourself up).
4. Pull up your hood, put in ear plugs, turn on the iPod, or do whatever else you feel you need to do. Some people have greater focusing ability with soft background nature sounds or music, or even a full-fledged guided visualization recording playing. Once again, this is a personal experience, so feel free to sample the choices. The goal is to quiet your mind and just BE. If you don't even know what I'm talking about there, just know that eventually, you will—and you'll like it.
5. Start noticing your breathing. You can experiment with different breath work, but if you only observe your natural pace, you are quite OK.

From here the choices are infinite. You can focus on a mantra or a sacred word; you can chant; or you can even focus your attention on different chakra points or parts of your body that might need extra energy. If you want to do some "level two" work, focus your attention on a point in the center of your head. If you are using a mantra, you may wish to repeat it 108 times, as the number 108 is a very auspicious number in many cultures. I use a Hindu prayer bead mala for counting. If you have a rosary, you can count around the circular part two times, as there are 54 beads on the circular garland part of the rosary.

Meditating is like going to the gym. At first, it feels like nothing is happening and you aren't getting anywhere, or you feel like your time is wasted. But eventually, you'll notice the changes.

If there is such a group near you, I would highly recommend joining a meditation group both to get a jump start on making a firm time commitment, and to up-level your practice more quickly. When you are in a group, you are literally helped up by the vibration of the group—very useful if you are struggling with meditating. There is definitely a reason why many people meditate in groups, so give them the opportunity to help you.

Meditating is a very counter-intuitive activity for busy people. While it seems logical that you will somehow have to "make up" the time you spend meditating, given enough time using this Spirit Server, you actually usually gain time. And beyond having more time, you won't sweat the small stuff as much, too. Eventually your life will seem more manageable in every way.

The Spiritual Writing Server

This Server takes the meditation strategy above and grounds it by writing down the wisdom you receive. It provides a way to tune in to the untapped universe of talent, wisdom, great thoughts, and total being-ness AND have the material notes for use later on. Remember, everything is one energy. So, the wisdom you seek is all always already there . . . or here . . . or everywhere, NOW! (For those of you who just got your mindset "religion-triggered," let me rename this "The Answer to Your Prayers" Server, as it is about writing your dialogue with your "Higher Power" as you understand It.) If you feel like you need to protect yourself before doing this ("energy follows thoughts"), first visualize yourself surrounded in holy light or white light, and intend a conversation only with your Higher Power.

I literally "tuned in" and used this very technique to write these next few paragraphs and a few other sections of this book I felt could use a little help from a "Higher Power." See if you think what follows sounds slightly different from the rest of my writing.

"Step into the caldron of quantum energy, as it will take you to places beyond your wildest dreams. Get a pen and notepad and follow this to-do list:

1. Believe it is possible and that there is helpful energy 'out there.'

2. Set your intention to align with helpful, high-vibrating guidance only. Think of it as dialing the 'spiritual telephone number' that you want. Some people choose to visualize themselves surrounded by a field of white or purple light as they set this intention.
3. Sit quietly and allow your thoughts to become quiet. Observe your breathing to center yourself if necessary. Some people put on soft background music, tones, or chants to drown out possible noises or distracting sounds.
4. Once quiet, start to listen to the conversation that is present around you.

   If you are a beginner, write long-hand as opposed to typing the information you receive. This higher-thinking game of 'cat and mouse, listen and learn' is how a great many minds have received their divine inspiration. It is all available to you if you wish to get present to the 'present' that is being offered.

   If you want an answer to a question or insight about a topic, hold the question or topic in your mind, and the higher spiritual energies that assist you will approach the conversation regarding that topic for your mind to develop with them. You do have a part in it all. Your mind connecting with ours is vital for easily and quickly becoming enlightened with new, fresh, bold ideas that you've never thought of before. Inspiration is just that: an injection of spiritual essence that has been captured by the person who was able to accept the gifts.
5. Write what is in your head. Write it word-for-word, even though you have no idea what the next word is going to be. The more you practice this, the easier it will become for you. Encourage children to do this, so they trust in the process throughout their lives. (Children seem to be able to capture this concept much more easily than adults.) A world that is

> THAT tapped-in is truly a world that has brought itself into a time and place of reverence for the divine energies."

So, there you have it. I literally did not have a clue what word was coming next as I typed the above paragraphs. I was in a relaxed state and just typed whatever words "popped into my head." As I said, I recommend hand-writing first and then working your way into typing. I say this because that was the way I was taught, AND because one day, long ego—er . . . I mean, long ago—when I was tired of writing, I decided (there's the first problem!) that I (hello there, ego!) wanted to type instead. I sat down at my computer all ready to go and got into my relaxed state, and then waited for the words. I felt the "hookup" and then got my fingers ready to type. And here's what came out onto the page as I typed each word, not knowing how the sentence would end: "You are not ready to type yet." Then my connection released. WHAT? Clearly I was getting a message from spirit, because it wasn't what I wanted to hear!

Many parts of my feng shui book *Move Your Stuff, Change Your Life* were written using this technique. What's funny is, sometimes people say to me how they used this or that feng shui cure, and I reply, "Oh, that's a good one—I'll have to remember that one!" And they say, "I got that from your book!" It was so "not me" that I didn't even remember writing it. I think this is how great symphonies and many other grand inventions came to be. They were divinely inspired (a.k.a. "in-spirited") messages from higher-vibrating realms.

If you can align yourself by modernizing your mind and clearing your unresourceful thoughts and beliefs, balancing your body in such a way as to be able to handle the high frequencies, and enhancing your environment so it allows you to make contact like this, you will always be able to rely on God, your intuition, higher-vibrating energies, Holy Spirit, higher consciousness (or whatever you want to call it that doesn't cause you to tweak out and need another Mind Modernizer!). You are not EVER alone, unless you want to take the physics perspective that

EVERYTHING IS ONE. And if that is so, you are merely allowing one part (a very wise part, I might add) of your universal energy body to express itself that does not usually get much air time.

> Many people find that the fuller the moon, the better they can "connect" in their meditation or spiritual writing. You may struggle one day and find it very easy to meditate or write on another—so stay with it!

The Giving and Receiving Server

WARNING: This particular Spirit Server also has a side effect: it can make you very financially wealthy. So, if material abundance isn't your thing, you might want to skip it. This "spiritual" technique, as challenging as it is for most people, is one of the easiest ways to manifest consistent and lasting financial freedom. This is my go-to technique when people say they want more prosperity as a part of their Dream Life.

For centuries, many have used this powerful technique to gain both spiritually and materially, because it was written up in the Bible. Others have taken it on without a conscious connection to religion or anything having to do with the Bible—it just occurred to them to do so. I am here to tell you that whether you see this as something "from the Bible" or not, it makes no difference with regard to the result. Here's the technique: if you give away 10% of your gross income to whatever recipient "feeds your soul or spirit," you will receive a multiple-fold return on that investment, contribution, or gift.

If you have figured out and overcome your false beliefs or limited, "lack" thinking with the Mind Modernizers, you've definitely climbed aboard the train to abundance. Now, if you want to stoke the engine to get on the fast track, try this simple yet profound technique. There really should not be any more to this discussion. It is clean and simple. But most everyone's ego immediately starts chattering with very rational reasons why you shouldn't apply it. So, let's start with a little science and energy background for those of you whose "you've-got-to-be-kidding" red flag just got raised.

In science, it is said that nature abhors a vacuum. Black holes in outer space pull "things" into themselves just as a home vacuum cleaner sucks in dust and dirt. If you create a vacuum with regard to your income, it can do nothing but pull more income toward the void—which is you! This is the same "space equals opportunity" rule that you learned from the clutter-clearing processes in Chapter 3, only here we're using it to specifically create financial abundance and the wonderful feeling of financial freedom that goes along with it.

I'm going to run over the concept again in case you are still hearing resistance "buzzing" in your head, because it is that important. As a matter of fact, if your mind is buzzing, stop and take a moment to write down the thoughts that might stop you from applying this strategy. Here are some of the usual ones that pop in:

- "Money is the root of all evil."
- "I don't deserve it."
- "I wouldn't know how to handle or manage money if I had a lot."
- "Having abundance in life is a curse."
- "Being wealthy is ostentatious."
- "Having money would make it hard to be in my family."
- "Wealth would cause chaos in my life."
- "Having more money would make me *feel* (body/ emotion) guilty (feng shui earth element), because others don't have as much."

Work your Mind Modernizers to clear out these or any other life-obstructing thoughts before moving on to the technique.

I know that although this method for gaining prosperity is simple, it is paradoxical. How is it possible that you GAIN wealth by GIVING a portion of your income away? The hidden ingredients are faith and action. You have to "surrender" and suspend doubt or disbelief to take the first step to get the reward.

Call it a cosmic game if you want, or think of it as a law just like the law of gravity. Assign a meaning to it that works for you, because it is just as real as gravity. I would actually say that there is "gravity" associated with your learning and applying this service, because if you do, others in the world will benefit, which will start to up-level the entire world's energy! "Let there be peace and abundance on Earth, and let it BEGIN WITH ME!" Can you imagine a world in which everyone was playing this game? This could be the key to world peace—because quite frankly, everyone is usually fighting over something that they want that "the other" has (very un-ecological and "un-faithful" thinking).

Let's get back to the technique again. See if you are more amenable to it now than when you started reading this section. Give away 10 percent of your gross income to whomever or whatever institution nourishes or grows your soul, spirit, or heart, *while being conscious of and willing to ponder or work through whatever buttons are being pushed as you do so,* and you will receive in return a minimum of 10 times the amount that you gave.

If the word *give* has got you all bunched up, re-frame it. Think of your financial *gift* as *payment* for the spiritual gift or soul growth you gained. Then, it is not giving at all—it is an energetically equivalent payback for *the gift YOU received.* Money is just a form of energy, after all. Faithfully *paying back for inner growth* is actually what you are really doing rather than just applying a method of releasing money to create a vacuum.

There was a time when money was a major struggle for me. I learned about this method and thought, "What have I got to lose? I hardly have anything anyway." (How's that for a good attitude?) But it was still hard. When I first started working this technique, I said to myself, "If I took this 10 percent that I worked so hard for and sent it to one of my creditors, then at least I would be that much less in debt." But by saying this sentence to myself, it showed that I believed I had to work for all the money I made, I didn't trust the universe to help me, and I felt certain I had to do it all myself. All of these thoughts needed to be cleansed from my mind, because the truth is, you don't have to do it all yourself, and you don't have to work hard for every dollar you make—unless you want to believe that. You see, if you have those thoughts, you are choosing to have faith in them. And *that faith* is what is getting you the lack of abundance you have now. This process is about putting faith in something that has a successful track record.

I eventually got the little ball rolling, and my finances grew and grew. I got the luscious opportunity of writing a book that became a best-seller. Then I began to make larger chunks of money in royalty checks. Oddly enough, it was and sometimes still is a far greater challenge for me to give away 10 percent now that I have some money than when I was broke (another paradox). I eventually figured out that for some reason, it is much easier for me to write 15 checks for $100 than one check for $1,500. That's just me. You might be different. It's a mind game—that's all. I discovered that it isn't about the amount. Ten percent is ten percent.

How hard was it for me to write and give that first check for $1,500, when I had way more than that in debt? HARD. VERY HARD. Did it feel crazy? Yes. Did it feel nauseating? Yes. Did it feel stupid? Did I feel stupid? Yes. Yes. Yes. Yes, a thousand times yes. But I did it anyway.

The series of conscious, mental gyrations that I went through to give that money away *was* the first serious welcoming of prosperity for me. It was so unsettling, it actually kept me up that night. I felt clutter release-type feelings ("I shouldn't have, but what if... blah, blah, blah"), only exponentially stronger. I heard my inner voice calling me stupid and illogical, and I certainly felt that way, too. I had a whole mind, body, spirit reboot going all at once. But I knew this law existed, because it had revealed itself to me in many smaller ways before.

I somehow knew it was really the only way to make the leap from scratching around and "doing it all myself" to "allowing the Universe to become my source for everything." I suddenly had the realization that I wasn't doing anything myself anyway. I was a tiny part of the universe, and I could not get out of it no matter how hard I tried! I had an unfamiliar feeling of surrender.

And just like when I VERY reluctantly let my son's high chair go at the garage sale that day, and then I eventually jumped up and down for the five dollars I received, my surrender turned into an excited anticipation. I felt childlike—like I knew Ed McMahon was on his way to my house with a lottery check or something—because I had just put myself on the fast track for financial opportunities.

Oh yeah, my mind still tries to fight me on this technique, by the way—even though it has **never** let me down. I still go through mental gyrations to this day—EVEN THOUGH IT HAS NEVER LET ME DOWN. No matter how many times I give away the money, it still feels illogical. The difference is that now, I am living a very comfortable life while I mentally gyrate! Yes, I have both the feelings of being illogical and financially stupid *and* having financial freedom at the same time. A paradox once again, but it's one I'd rather live with than the old, heavy feelings of insurmountable debt I had when I was "in charge."

It is helpful to shift your perception from "all the money I make is mine, and anything I give makes me have less" to "all the money I receive is a gift from the Universe, and it is no big deal to give 10 percent of a gift away." It helps me, anyway.

Imagine that every financially rewarding connection you make is because of the work done by your "secret universal tithing agent." Wouldn't you expect to pay an agent for his or her connections?

Here's my process in a nutshell: I receive some money, I calculate 10 percent, I think and wrestle with my false notions about money, I declare them invalid even though they are pushing my buttons, I acknowledge someone or some organization that feeds my soul or lifts my spirit, and I surrender to the paradoxical and illogical nature of the technique. And then I give the money anyway.

By the way, if you're giving 10 percent and are truly OK with it, or if you give and don't "mentally gyrate or squirm," you may have completed working through all of your false beliefs about money on one particular level. I'd suggest giving more than 10 percent to see if you hit any hidden inner thoughts that still need work.

Here's a to-do list to engage with this technique if you need one for quick reference:

1. Write down every speck of income you receive in your notebook on a page entitled, "Formula for Creating Financial Abundance: Give 10 Percent of All Gross Income Away to Anyone or Any Institution that Feeds My Spirit, Soul, or Heart."
2. Choose a regular and consistent time to calculate 10 percent of your income. If you receive one paycheck per month, then perhaps once a month will work for you. If you receive many checks, tips, or other types of income throughout the week, then you may want to calculate your percentage weekly. With my particular business, my income fluctuates week to week. And since I figured out that it was easier for me to write 10 $40 checks than one $400 check in the beginning, I write checks every time I acquire any income from anyone.
3. Give away (*pay*) your 10 percent to whomever or whatever institution teaches you something about yourself, feeds your soul, nourishes your heart, or otherwise helps you grow. If you choose to give to (*pay*) a charity, be sure that something that charity does touches your soul and uplifts you. If not,

be creative and look elsewhere for the recipients to whom you might offer your monetary support. Perhaps no one else understands your giving choices but you—that's OK. They don't have to. It's your choice and no one else's. Just be conscious of your giving acts, and you'll see the vacuum law work for you.

4. Take a moment each time you give to listen to the voice inside. See what it is struggling with and acknowledge it. Reassure it that you are moving forward with faith, if nothing else. If you have to, tell yourself that you are choosing to do something different in order to create a different financial outcome for yourself—even if you are not fully aware of how or why it works. In other words, use the same approach that we used in the other parts of this book: "fake it until you make it." Scientists have proven that if you smile—even if you are faking it—your body's chemistry responds favorably. In the "receiving abundance" world, fake it by giving, even if you have reservations about doing so. Be conscious that you have reservations, and determine that you are going to give anyway. This sets up a type of surrender and attaches energy that is allied with *faith* to your actions.
5. Now that you've given away a part of your income, spend time feeling a childlike feeling of anticipation. Do whatever you feel like you would do if you were handed your supreme Dream Life on a silver platter. Jump up and down flailing your arms while you scream for joy, if that's your style, or close your eyes and give thanks quietly. Your attitude should exude that the universe is pulling out all the stops to make you happy. The more you can practice feeling this, the more happiness you'll find flowing your way. The universe will make the connection between your current conditions and your Dream Life, and it will fill in the gap with the money to achieve your dreams.

6. Get in touch with feelings of gratitude when ANY income comes your way. And then repeat this process.

Have I run over this concept enough times yet to get you to act or even experiment with the process? I hope so!

Generating an Abundance of Time

I have also noticed that the Giving and Receiving Server works just as well for generating time as it does for generating money. So, if your dream is a cleared calendar to write a novel, illustrate a children's book, or hike the John Muir Trail, then create a vacuum in your calendar by working with this giving to receive principle. How? Consciously give away your time. Perform selfless service. If you need 10 free hours, volunteer for an hour. Volunteer preferably somewhere that really feeds your soul (it usually does), just like you give the money away to recipients that uplift you. Once again, this approach is counterintuitive, I know—but try it. You'll see that there's a vacuum law.

As with giving money, this process works best if you suspend or give up the notion that you are separate from the laws of the universe. So, get in the back seat and let the law of giving and receiving drive for a while. You might like where you end up!

The Heed the Call and Surrender the Dream Server

Sheesh—there sure was a lot of surrendering in the Giving to Receive Server! But that was a warm-up compared to this one. The phrase from *The Gambler* song comes to mind because when I think of it, well . . . "You got to know when to hold 'em, know when to fold 'em." This server is about heeding the call from your (fill in your favorite word for Higher Power here) and surrendering your Dream Outcome to make a drab life fab. Yep. Give it up. Take a deep breath and release it.

Let me give you examples from my own life for this one. Back in the late 80's and early 90's, my Dream Outcome was to get some decent landscape architecture work. That's it—pretty simple. I had had my own design practice for years and always felt like I was "getting nowhere," no matter how good or bad the economy was. (There's the hint: if you don't feel in the flow, there's probably some Mind Modernizing and Environment Enhancing to do at the very least!) I had never taken the time to clear out poor-quality thoughts like, "women can't get ahead in the building industry," or to investigate at all what would happen if I changed careers (using the Four Questions for Clarity Modernizer). I erroneously *thought* "it was my lot in life" to be a landscape architect, because that was the degree I got from college. (That's dangerous, uninvestigated thinking for sure!)

In the midst of all this early 90's cruddy thinking, I got married, bought a house, and started doing some feng shui cures on my home. That little bit of feng shui effort got me a call from an editor at Simon and Schuster to write a book for them. (Oh yeah, I'm getting in the flow—I didn't pitch them at all. I simply paid attention to the opportunity when it presented itself, without letting thoughts like "I'm not a writer—I'm a landscape architect!" stop me.)

Then life threw me another curve ball. I got pregnant. I thought I was in a happy marriage, so that should have been a good thing, right? I thought I should be jumping for joy, but instead, it FREAKED ME OUT! (Low-vibrating emotion.) I went from a confident business owner and new-found writer to a scared, vulnerable, "how the hell does that come out of there?" and "how am I going to keep a design firm afloat, do a book promo tour, AND take care of this baby?" hot mess! Looking back with the 20/20 vision of hindsight, I can see that the tracks needed to change, even though I was totally and ever-optimistically thinking I could make my struggling design business work without changing my beliefs or environment. (Duh! If you always do what you've always done, you'll always get what you've always gotten!)

So, being the too-morning-sick-to-go-to-work gal that I was (I was fine until the second trimester, when my doc guilt-tripped me into taking pharmaceutical prenatal vitamins instead of continuing the natural things I was doing), I let go of how I needed to make a living and decided (committed) to take year to write *Move Your Stuff, Change Your Life.* My husband was not on board with this idea, as it sounded like a big money loser to him—that was HIS mindset stuff, which luckily I did not buy.

Thanks to my previously "worst thing to happen that turned into the best thing" death experience, I easily got "in the flow" with tons of new, fresh, and exciting feng shui cures that were "given to me" from the other side to put into the book. (Seriously folks, no embodied soul taught me most of the feng shui cures and rituals in that book!) And guess what? That book has paid me *way* more than I would have earned doing landscape architecture that year. Score so far: surrendering, one—doing the same thing over again, zero.

Fast forward to today. My career has never felt more right. I LOVE helping people, I LOVE doing teleseminars, and I LOVE speaking events, too! If the landscape architecture thing had been going well, I might not have ever taken a chance, and I might not have these fun and exciting opportunities and events in my life today!

All of this leads me to what's going on in my life right now. Just like my life got overhauled when I wrote *Move Your Stuff,* my life is completely changing tracks as I write this book. During the entire process of writing this book, I got divorced. Yes, the more I feng shuied, energy transferred, Helpful People-boxed, meditated, etc. for a loving, trustworthy, passionate, intimate, fun relationship, the worse the one I had with my husband kept getting, and the more I felt "a calling" to get divorced.

I sure am glad I have seen the premise "it's always good in the end, and if it's not good now, it's just not the end" in action before, because this was a tough one. Hats off to other divorcées who have kept their jobs and kids going during all that a divorce entails—it took just about all I had. I TOTALLY took a leap of faith that I was supposed to start the divorce process, even though I had no idea what was going to happen next. The "divine discontent" calling was strong to do so; it was like I would be universally nagged to death if I didn't. If you feel like no matter where you hide, you can't escape the nagging, I'd say that's a calling.

My egoic mind said, "The feng shui queen gets divorced? Ooh, no . . . THAT'S not good for business!" The inner child said, "I'm too scared to go through that door!" My digestive system said, "For God's sake—do it!" My spirit said, "You are not your body, mind, or thoughts. You are an infinite being, and so is he. It's all an illusion anyway, so just surrender to what is." I'm telling you, I was all over the place.

But even as I write this, having just gone through the most tumultuous year of my life relationship-wise, I can honestly say that my husband was a great teacher of many valuable bits of wisdom that I would never have received if not for the years of turbulent times. I don't know the reason for the lessons in full yet, but I trust they'll be shown to me, just like the death experience gems eventually were.

And since the divorce is done, I have to say, my physical and mental health feels like it has shifted for the better. My spirit also feels like it is finally on the right track, after having felt stifled for decades. And, what has happened to my home since the divorce? It has finally recovered from the emotional "turbulence" that comes with a breakup. (Remember, your home is a reflection of what's going on in your life.) Since water is linked to emotions, "turbulence" showed up in my home during the divorce. The irrigation controller broke and stopped irrigating the yard; the fountain started leaking (water running free because of a leak is like house tears); two toilets were not turning off after flushing; and the kitchen sink clogged. These were the house mimicking my "on and off again" flow of emotions. Can you see how everything is tied together?

Through great pressure, diamonds are made.

Instead of thinking of a divorce—or whatever is going on in your life—as negative, look at it as a "life seed" that just got planted now and that will surely grow into something beautiful in the future. Hopefully, you'll be patient enough to see what blooms. (Keep getting your shifts together!) Like a seed, during tough times you also get plunged deep down into the depths of underground darkness before you eventually crack open, transform, and grow into something unique, beautiful, and different. It's just part of the process—in the same way that in order to jump very high, you have to start out by bending down way low. Both the down and the up are one event: the yin and yang of change.

So, if your Dream Outcome is fighting you like a bucking bronco, maybe you need to heed the call and surrender it to REALLY find that fab life you've been seeking. Even though I'm barely out of the woods with this divorce, I know that I am exactly where I'm supposed to be. I trusted my gut, and "the universal nagging" has quieted. Be open to the signs and signals and callings that just may lead you to a place far beyond what you wrote for your current Dream Outcome. Listen to your Higher Power—your soul, your destiny, the Universal Flow, whatever you want to call it—*AND* actually have the faith to act upon what you hear, and you'll taste the sweetness of life like I did. Hopefully, you've practiced enough techniques in this book to see the value in making this move.

Breathe . . . breathe . . . you are exactly where you are supposed to be.

Thanks, Universe.

Epilogue

We Are the World

I know I've mentioned it multiple times, but in case you need a little more motivation to keep your shifts together, remember, we're all really one energy. There is a game my son and I played when he was young that speaks to this connection. We would take turns holding up our index fingers in space while saying something like, "I'm touching Mars!" or "I'm touching the Great Wall of China!" or "I'm touching you!" We would continue by saying something like, "I'm touching a molecule of air that is touching other air that is touching the floor that is touching your chair that is touching you" (or whatever else it needed to touch to get to whatever we said we were touching).

It's a quirky game for sure, but it demonstrates the concept that "everything is connected." Sorry. You can try to escape, but in this little game, I can touch you anywhere you go! We've been programmed and socialized to think of ourselves as separate. But what if instead of learning that "you are this, not that," we all learned that "we are this AND that?"

Now, having said that, can you see how one person's lack-oriented thinking affects everyone else? We're all connected in this "universal blob of energy" and cannot escape. It follows, then, that if you are one of those out there who is slowing down your potential with limited thinking, you're slowing us all down! And as the unofficial spokesperson for world prosperity, I say, "Stop it!"

As you can see, if everyone cleaned up their unresourceful thoughts, de-cluttered and created thriving, ecologically conscious environments, tended to their physical bodies, and connected with their higher consciousness or spirit, the world would be a much different place.

Shift your thoughts from "Why is there hunger or terror?" with no action to "I use negativity in the world as my wake-up call to act. I am a part of the whole, and by 'doing my part,' modernizing my mind, enhancing my environment, balancing my body, and serving my spirit, I am positively affecting the whole." Your "singular" acts really do affect the whole!

Now, as the unofficial spokesperson for world abundance, peace, and freedom, I would like to be the first to say, "Thanks for doing your part!"

Well, there you have it—my favorite ways to create happy homes and humans. Your notebook should be full of ideas for creating a happier and healthier you right now! I'm sure that if you choose to use any or all of the ideas and techniques that you wrote down, you'll be propelled toward your intended life goals and will find yourself in a more consistent state of happiness and well-being.

Whatever you got from this book is exactly what you needed to receive at this time. But times change, and so will you. So, place this book and your notebook somewhere easily accessible, and you'll always have a resource as your life changes around you. Remember, this is an ongoing process—not a one-time thing.

If any chapter in the book was especially challenging for you, review it again now or make a note in your calendar to review it later. See if it makes more sense the second time around, now that you have completed the entire book.

Create a timeline for completing the changes in your notebook, if you feel it will help. Feng shui your home at a pace that intuitively feels right for you—and remember to track your changes in your notebook and take "after" photos. Once you compare them with the "before pictures" that you have already taken, you should have a new motivator to help you keep shifting.

If you don't think you'll use this book again in the next year, give it to a friend or sell it at your de-cluttering garage sale. Don't let this book become clutter in your home.

In the beginning of this book, I asked you to write down your dreams. It is time to reveal mine. It is my passion in life to use the tools that I have so graciously been given to take action to create a world that is perceived as better by everyone—one mind, body, spirit, home, or office at a time.

Imagine a world where every visible and invisible square inch has been mindfully tended to create peace, harmony, growth, and love. My wish is that as generations come and go, the wisdom to create sacred inner and outer space is passed on, and that this power is known and freely used by all. That's my dream. Thank you for being a part of it.

If you would like additional information about me or my work—or if you would like to comment on this book—please visit my web site: *www.MakeAShiftChangeYourLife.com*.

End Notes

Chapter 2

1. David R. Hawkins, *Power vs. Force* (Carlsbad, CA: Hay House, 2012).
2. Esther and Jerry Hicks, *Ask and It is Given* (Carlsbad, CA: Hay House, 2004). See Chapter 22 for the Abraham-Hicks representation of the Emotional Guidance Scale.
3. Esther and Jerry Hicks expand upon this point in Hicks, *Ask and It is Given*, particularly Chapter 22 and following.
4. These questions are attributed to Rene Descartes (Latinized name: *Carteisus*) and used widely throughout the psychotherapeutic approach of neuro-linguistic programming (NLP). For further discussion, see the work of NLP practitioners including Christopher Howard, *Leadership and Coaching Academy Master RESULTS Certification Training Manual* (Manhattan Beach, CA: Christopher Howard, 2006).
5. Bruce Lipton, *The Biology of Belief* (Carlsbad, CA: Hay House, 2005), 105.

Chapter 3

1. For helpful strategies and a more in-depth description, see Regina Leeds, *The 8-Minute Organizer* (Boston: Da Capo Press, 2012), especially page xiv.
2. American Physiological Society, "Losing Sleep Undoes the Rejuvenating Effects New Learning Has on the Brain," (Bethesda, MD: American Physiological Society, 2006), accessed August 11, 2013, http://www.eurekalert.org/pub_releases/2006-01/aps-lsu010506.php.

Chapter 4

1. For more detailed information on how to get specific needs met, check out Alison Armstrong's work at www.understandmen.com.
2. U.S. Environmental Protection Agency, 2002.
3. International Institute for Bau-Biology and Ecology, *Course 101 Workbook* (Santa Fe: International Institute for Bau-Biology and Ecology, 2007), 54.
4. My favorite in-depth book on this subject is B. C. Wolverton, *How to Grow Fresh Air* (New York: Penguin Books, 1997).
5. U.S. Environmental Protection Agency, *The Inside Story: A Guide to Indoor Air Quality* (Washington, DC: EPA, 2012).
6. American Lung Association, *Lung Disease Data* (Washington, DC: American Lung Association, 2006).
7. World Health Organization, *Water Quality and Health Strategy, 2013-2020* (Geneva, Switzerland: World Health Organization, 2013), Section 3.11.

8. The entire, fully detailed list can be found in Feng Shui Design, Academy of Healing Nutrition, *Practical Cooking with Melanie Ferreira: Cooking and Healing with the Longevity Diet* (New York: Academy of Healing Nutrition, 2006), 1–5.

9. See, for example, D.R. Crapper, S.S. Krishnan, and A. J. Dalton, "Brain Aluminum Distribution in Alzheimer's Disease and Experimental Neurofibrillary Degeneration," *Science* 180 (1973): 511–513; C.N. Martyn et al., "Geographical Relation Between Alzheimer's Disease and Aluminium in Drinking Water," *The Lancet* 1 (1989): 59–62; and K.G. McGrath, "An Earlier Age of Breast Cancer Diagnosis Related to More Frequent Use of Antiperspirants/ Deodorants and Underarm Shaving," *European Journal of Cancer* 12 (2003): 479–485.

10. For a more in-depth description of Yin and Yang foods, see Academy of Healing Nutrition, *Food Energetics with Roger Green Course Manual* (New York: Academy of Healing Nutrition, 2006).

11. See also Academy of Healing Nutrition, *Food Energetics with Roger Green Course Manual.*

12. An in-depth analysis of these elements can be found in Academy of Healing Nutrition, *Food Energetics with Roger Green Course Manual.*

13. These products are available through online retailers, including The EMF Safety Shop at www.lessemf.com.

Resources

MIND

Hawkins, David R. *Power Versus Force*. Carlsbad, CA: Hay House, 2012.

Hicks, Esther and Jerry. *Ask and It is Given*. Carlsbad, CA: Hay House, 2004.

Howard, Christopher. *Leadership and Coaching Academy Master RESULTS Certification Training Manual*. Manhattan Beach, CA: Christopher Howard, 2006.

Lipton, Bruce. *The Biology of Belief*. Carlsbad, CA: Hay House, 2005.

PAX Programs Incorporated: www.understandmen.com.

Rock House Global: www.rockhouseglobal.com.

Vaknin, Shlomo. *The Big Book of NLP Techniques*. Woodland Hills, CA: Inner Patch Publishing, 2011.

ENVIRONMENT

American Physiological Society. "Losing Sleep Undoes the Rejuvenating Effects New Learning Has on the Brain." Bethesda, MD: American Physiological Society, 2006. Accessed August 11, 2013. http://www.eurekalert.org/pub_releases/2006-01/aps-lsu010506.php.

Carter, Karen Rauch. *Move Your Stuff, Change Your Life*. New York: Simon & Schuster, 2000.

International Institute for Building-Biology and Ecology: www.hbelc.org.

Kennedy, David Daniel. *Feng Shui for Dummies*. New York: Hungry Minds, Inc., 2001.

Kingston, Karen. *Clear Your Clutter with Feng Shui*. New York: Broadway Books, 1999/

Laporte, Paula Baker, Erica Elliott, M.D., and John Banta. *Prescriptions for a Healthy House*. British Columbia, Canada: New Society Publishers, 2001.

Leeds, Regina. *The 8 Minute Organizer*. Boston: Da Capo Press, 2012.

Linn, Denise. *Sacred Space*. New York: Ballantine Books, 1995.

Thompson, Athena. *Homes that Heal*. British Columbia, Canada: New Society Publishers, 2004.

BODY

Academy of Healing Nutrition. *Food Energetics with Roger Green Course Manual*. New York: Academy of Healing Nutrition, 2006.

Crapper, D.R., S.S. Krishnan, and A.J. Dalton. "Brain Aluminum Distribution in Alzheimer's Disease and Experimental Neurofibrillary Degeneration." *Science* 180 (1973): 511–513.

Feng Shui Design, Academy of Healing Nutrition. *Practical Cooking with Melanie Ferreira: Cooking and Healing with the Longevity Diet*. New York: Academy of Healing Nutrition, 2006.

Hay, Louise. *You Can Heal Your Life*. Carlsbad, CA: Hay House, 1984.

International Institute for Bau-Biology and Ecology. *Course 101 Workbook*. Santa Fe: International Institute for Bau-Biology and Ecology, 2007.

Lipton, Bruce. *The Biology of Belief*. Carlsbad, CA: Hay House, 2005.

Martyn, C.N., C. Osmond, J.A. Edwardson, D.J.P. Barker, E.C. Harris, and R.F. Lacey. "Geographical Relation Between Alzheimer's Disease and Aluminium in Drinking Water." *The Lancet* 1 (1989): 59–62.

McGrath, K.G. "An Earlier Age of Breast Cancer Diagnosis Related to More Frequent Use of Antiperspirants/Deodorants and Underarm Shaving." *European Journal of Cancer* 12 (2003): 479–485.

Reichstein, Gail. *Wood Becomes Water: Chinese Medicine in Everyday Life*. New York: Kodansha International, 1998.

U.S. Environmental Protection Agency. *The Inside Story: A Guide to Indoor Air Quality*. Washington, DC: EPA, 2012.

Wolverton, B.C. *How to Grow Fresh Air*. New York: Penguin Books, 1997.

World Health Organization. *Water Quality and Health Strategy, 2013-2020*. Geneva, Switzerland: World Health Organization, 2013.

SPIRIT

Dyer, Wayne W. *The Power of Intention*. Carlsbad, CA, Hay House, 2004.

Grabhorn, Lynn. *Excuse Me, Your Life is Waiting: The Astonishing Power of Feelings*. Charlottesville, VA: Hampton Roads, 2000.

Hicks, Esther and Jerry. *Getting into the Vortex*. Carlsbad, CA Hay House, 2010.

Michael, Todd. *The Twelve Conditions of a Miracle*. New York, Tarcher Penguin, 2004.

Roman, Sanaya, and Duane Packer. *Opening to Channel.* Tiburon, CA, HJ Kramer Inc., 1987.

About the Author

Karen Rauch Carter is a professional feng shui consultant, healthy-lifestyle designer, international speaker, and licensed landscape architect. She has studied with many teachers on various subjects including feng shui, design, dowsing, yoga, food energetics, neuro-linguistic repatterning, and alternative energy healing, to name a few. Her feng shui book, *Move Your Stuff, Change Your Life* (New York: Simon & Schuster, 2000) is a national best-seller that has been translated into several languages.

How to Contact Karen Rauch Carter

Karen has more helpful information and a variety of products, programs, and services available to assist you on her website, including teaching others to become professional feng shui consultants and healthy-lifestyle designers. She can be contacted at www.MakeAShiftChangeYourLife.com.

Send Your Shift Success Stories!

Many people who are stuck in fear or who have lost the ability to dream have begun trusting in feng shui and the various other techniques found in this book because they have read someone else's success story. If you'd like to toot your own horn about your shifts and pay it forward to the world, send your story and written permission to info@KarenRauchCarter.com. You may then be featured in Karen's newsletter or in an upcoming blog post! The readers thank you in advance!